ELVIS

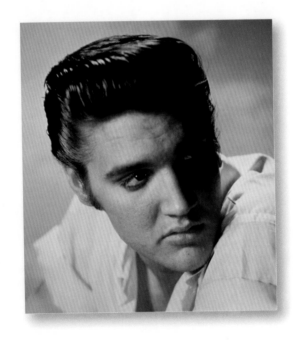

ELVIS

Susie Behar

igloo

igloo

Published in 2011 by
Igloo Books Ltd.
Cottage Farm
Sywell
NN6 OBJ
www.igloo-books.com

10 9 8 7

ISBN 978-1-84817-400-9

Designed by The Bridgewater Book Company

Printed and manufactured in China

Contents

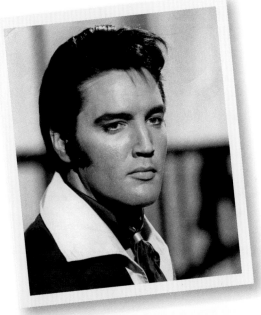

INTRODUCTION

"I ain't no saint, but I've tried never to do anything that would hurt my family or offend God ... I figure all any kid needs is hope and the feeling he or she belongs. If I could do or say anything that would give some kid that feeling, I would believe I had contributed something to the world."

ELVIS, INTERVIEW IN THE FIFTIES

Elvis Presley is known as the King of rock 'n' roll and the most successful recording artist in musical history. Not only was he the first rock star, he was a hugely gifted and charismatic singer with enormous vocal ability. He was also a talented actor and, last but not least, an icon worshiped by hundreds of thousands of fans the world over.

Brought up in poverty in the southern United States in Tupelo, Mississippi, Elvis spoke with a southern drawl, behaved in public with the impeccable manners of a southern gentleman and, as his parents had taught him, addressed people as "sir" or "madam"—and this included members of the press. He also ate a southern diet, rich in fat and sweet foods. He always remembered where he came from and had, according to friends, an inferiority complex. Nevertheless, throughout his life, Elvis retained a sense of decency toward those around him, in particular his fans. He hated to let them down and, despite often being exhausted, would talk to them after his concerts and have his picture taken with them. When they swarmed at the gates of his Memphis home, Graceland, he would take the time to meet them and sign autographs.

OPPOSITE *Elvis performs outdoors on a small stage to the adulation of a young crowd, 1956.*

RIGHT *Elvis signing autographs when he arrives in Los Angeles to start filming* Love Me Tender, *August 16, 1956.*

ABOVE *Elvis confers with Colonel Tom Parker on the set of* Change Of Habit, *around 1969.*

OPPOSITE *Elvis kissing a fan on the cheek after a performance at the Florida Theater in St Petersburg, Florida, 7 August, 1961.*

Elvis was catapulted to fame in the fifties by a series of rock 'n' roll hits released by Sun Records in Memphis. His records became a cultural phenomenon that reverberated throughout the Western world and, in some cases, beyond. He was only 19 at the time, uneducated, and deeply attached to his family. In particular, he had a extremely close relationship with his mother, Gladys. When Elvis was a child, Gladys hardly ever let him out of her sight; when he became famous, she couldn't bear the separations that resulted from his touring and recordings stints. They had their own private language and relied heavily upon each other. When Elvis whipped up press controversy over his unorthodox hip swiveling and leg shaking moves, Gladys was terrified that someone might harm her boy. Some argue that Elvis' fame ironically led to her premature death at the age of 46 from a heart attack. Those who knew him said that when Gladys died, Elvis was never the same again.

One of the many mysteries of Elvis' career was the power that he relinquished to one man to whom he was famously loyal and trusting. His manager, Colonel Parker, led Elvis down roads that may not have been the best for him, either personally or professionally. He also exploited him at every opportunity. That Elvis never broke free is extraordinary and remains an unsolved puzzle. The Colonel put Elvis in the movies, but, in many cases, they were the wrong movies. After nearly a decade of movies with sometimes bad songs and even worse plots, the Colonel finally realized that things had to change, and Elvis embarked on one of the most successful comebacks in music history. For a few heady years, he was the "King" again.

However, by this time, Elvis had come to rely on prescription drugs taken to help him to sleep and to stay awake and to lose weight. He became addicted, without ever fully realizing it. From the mid-seventies he was in a downward spiral, from which he never escaped. He died in 1977 at the age of 42.

His fans never stopped loving him and some can't accept that he is dead. There is a theory that he faked his own death to escape the fame and that he is still alive today. Of course, this is fanciful, but it shows how extraordinarily powerful the man was and the icon still is, and the unique place he holds in the minds and imagination of his public.

Elvis also has a unique place in music history for another reason. He remains one of the best-selling recording artists of all time; throughout his life he broke many records for sales of singles and albums, and concert attendances.

This books charts his rise to success, his years in the movies on the path to possible obscurity, and his amazing comeback in 1968. It tracks his eventual decline after a few more years at the height of his powers. It also looks at his relationships, loves, and friendships, musical and otherwise. As an explanatory note, the movies are listed in chronological order of shooting, and the featured records are also listed chronologically by release date.

1935–1948
FROM TUPELO
TO MEMPHIS

Elvis Aaron Presley was born in East Tupelo, Northern Mississippi, at around 4 o'clock in the morning on January 8, 1935, to Vernon and Gladys Presley. Thirty minutes before his birth, his identical twin brother Jesse Garon (the middle names of the twins were chosen because they rhymed) was stillborn. Jesse was buried in an unmarked grave the following day; Elvis always mourned his loss.

The twins were delivered in their parents' two-room "shotgun" shack (so-called because if you fired a gun through one wall it would exit the other), which had been built by Vernon, his father, just before Elvis was born. Welfare paid for the physician who attended Elvis' birth.

Before her pregnancy, Gladys had been a machine operator at the Tupelo Garment Factory and Vernon had a variety of jobs, including that of a milkman and a truck driver. The couple had met through their church and had eloped when Vernon was just 17 and Gladys, 22. The underage Vernon added two years to his age on the marriage certificate to ensure that the marriage was legal.

Elvis Presley was a child of the culture, music, and evangelical religion of the deep South. The town of Tupelo took its name from the Tupelo gum trees that were once common throughout the area. A typically poor southern town, it was home to farmers, sharecroppers, and factory workers and, in the 1930s, a small community of bootleggers.

Once the home of the native Chickasaw tribe, who lived in its woods and valley, Tupelo was the scene of fierce fighting between the Confederate and Union soldiers in the Civil War. The town had to be rebuilt after the conflict, and was then rescued from obscurity by two railroads, the Mobile and Ohio and the St Louis and San Francisco, which brought industry in the form of a Carnation milk plant, three textile plants, and a cotton mill. In 1936, Tupelo became the first city in the nation to acquire electrical power. This was provided by the Tennessee Valley Authority.

Beyond the intersection of the two railroads, just past the main streets of the city, lay Shakerag, the African-American section. Beyond this was East Tupelo—literally on the wrong side of the tracks. In the 1930s, it had a schoolhouse, a grocery store, the First Assembly of God Church, and clusters of mostly small two-roomed houses. It was in one of these houses that Elvis Presley was born.

Did You Know?

Elvis Presley's roots went way back in the South. His great-great-great grandfather was William Mansell (1795–1842), a settler in western Tennesee. His great-great-great grandmother was Morning White Dove (1800–1835), a member of the Cherokee tribe.

OPPOSITE *The house where Elvis was born in East Tupelo, Mississippi, 1935.*

Elvis' EARLY LIFE

> "There were times we had nothing to eat but cornbread and water ... but we always had compassion for people. Poor we were, I'll never deny that. But trash we weren't ... We never had any prejudice. We never put anybody down. Neither did Elvis."
>
> VERNON PRESLEY
> (TAKEN FROM GURALNICK, *LAST TRAIN TO MEMPHIS*)

It was the time of the Great Depression and the Presleys were poor, living only just above the breadline. But they were a close family and Elvis was much loved throughout his childhood. Extended family on both sides lived in Tupelo and Elvis said in later life that, although his childhood had been difficult, the family values that he learned in Tupelo were the ones he always attempted to live by.

When Elvis was just three years old, the already struggling family suffered a further blow when Vernon was found guilty of forging a check. He had sold a hog and falsified the amount on the check. He was given a three-year jail sentence, though he served only eight months. In his absence, the young Elvis became closer to his mother, who adored and pampered him. After Vernon's release, poverty forced the family to move from one rented house to another, ending up even closer to Shakerag, where Elvis would have been exposed to the sounds of rhythm and blues.

When he was ten years old, his teacher asked him to compete in a talent contest at the Mississippi–Alabama Fair and Dairy Show. Dressed in a cowboy outfit, he sang Red Foley's "Old Shep," a sentimental country song about a boy and his dog. He won a prize (Elvis later recalled that he came fifth)—a free ticket to all the rides.

On his next birthday, he received a guitar from his parents, though he had actually asked for a bicycle (Gladys thought a bicycle was too dangerous), and his uncle, Vester, began to give him basic guitar lessons. Elvis and his guitar became an item; he frequently took it to school, where he gave impromptu recitals, though there is no indication that these were in any way outstanding.

Did You Know?

Elvis adored comic books as a child. He said he always imagined himself to be the hero.

OPPOSITE *Tupelo, Mississippi, 1938.*
BELOW *Elvis with his parents, Gladys and Vernon, 1938.*

first musical influences:
COUNTRY
& GOSPEL

In Tupelo, Elvis and his family regularly attended the First Assembly of God Church, where gospel singing was a large part of the Pentecostal service. There are varying accounts by friends and relatives as to whether or not Elvis distinguished himself by his singing in church, but there is no doubt that gospel was his first love. His backing groups during his career, the Jordanaires and, later, the Stamps, were originally gospel quartets.

Elvis also grew up surrounded by the sounds of country music. He listened to local radio stations and his first musical hero was a family friend, Mississippi Slim (real name Carvel Lee Ausborn), a hillbilly singer with a radio show on Tupelo's WELO. Presley performed occasionally on one of Slim's shows, *The Black and White Jamboree*, an amateur hour held and broadcast every Saturday afternoon at the Lee County Courthouse. The young Elvis hung around the station to hear Slim as often as he could.

Living so close to Shakerag, Elvis would have been aware of blues music. Indeed, his first record (see page 29) was a cover of one of his blues heroes, Arthur Crudup. But it wasn't only country, gospel, and blues that Elvis loved. In an interview in the 1970s, he recalled that as a schoolboy he had listened to Mario Lanza and Dean Martin and music from the Metropolitan Opera. As Elvis said in later life "I just like music."

RIGHT TOP *Mario Lanza, taken around 1950.*

RIGHT *Hank Williams, taken in the 1950s.*

OPPOSITE *The nineteen-year-old Elvis in 1954.*

the move to
MEMPHIS

"the home of the blues"

As life got harder and harder for the Presleys in Tupelo—Vernon could rarely find work—the family decided to move to Memphis in search of something better. It was 1948 and, according to Elvis, they packed a truck with their belongings and left in the middle of the night. They could afford only the most basic housing until a year after their move, when they were accepted on a government-funded scheme and given accommodation at Lauderdale Heights. The two-room apartment was far more pleasant than their previous homes in Memphis. Vernon found work at the United Paint Company and Gladys sewed curtains.

Lauderdale Heights wasn't too far away from Beale Street and Elvis spent his teenage years around the area, absorbing the music and culture. He would have been well aware of the local blues singer and disc jockey, the legendary BB King (the "BB" stood for the "Beale Street Blues Boy"). It was in Memphis that Elvis first attended the all-night gospel singing sessions at the Ellis Auditorium that he later recalled in interviews in the 1970s.

BEALE STREET

Beale Street, in downtown Memphis, is nearly two miles (3 km) long, running from the Mississippi to East Street. Because of its proximity to the river, it became a popular place for black traders. By the 1860s, it had attracted many black musicians and, by the early 1900s, the street was filled with clubs, restaurants, and stores. Today, the blues clubs and restaurants are major tourist attractions. In 1977, Beale Street was officially declared "the home of the blues" by an act of Congress.

RIGHT *Elvis in Memphis, 1954.*

OPPOSITE *Beale Street in Memphis, 1965.*

Elvis at HUMES HIGH SCHOOL

In 1948, Elvis may have appeared superficially to be like any other poor kid attending Humes High School in Memphis: he played football and the guitar, paid only scant attention to his teachers, and worked part time on weekends. What is interesting is that not many of his classmates really remembered him all that well. They recall a quiet, shy boy, with a peculiar style of clothing. Rather than jeans, a T-shirt, and a crew cut, Elvis wore loud clothes (he had a preference for pink jackets) and his hair was heavily greased into a ducktail. They also remember his guitar playing, though nobody seemed that impressed until he played at a school talent show in the year he graduated. He was also considered to be a bit of a mother's boy—not helped by Gladys' habit of walking him to school until he was 15.

The first time Elvis was really noticed was in April 1953 at the Humes talent show. His recital went down a storm. As one classmate remembered, " … he sung his heart … the ovation was long and thunderous" (Dwight Malone, quoted on the Humes High School Reunion website).

In 1953, Elvis graduated from Humes High School and promptly took a job at MB Parker Machinists' Shop. He was the first person in his family to graduate from high school.

RED WEST

One of Elvis' friends at high school was Red West, who later became part of the Memphis Mafia. At school, West saved Elvis from having his longish hair cut by some other school kids. He became Elvis' driver, and later one of his bodyguards and a lifelong friend. A talented man in his own right, he wrote several songs for Elvis, including "Separate Ways."

ABOVE *Elvis in his high school Reserve Officers' Training Corps (ROTC) uniform, 1955.*

the *first love:*
DIXIE LOCK

"I don't think there was a whole lot of money involved in it. In the first weeks and months it was more like hometown boy makes good. He was still just totally innocent and spontaneous. There wasn't a proud or conceited bone in his body."

DIXIE LOCKE, *MEMPHIS PRESS* ARTICLE, 2004

Elvis hadn't had any real girlfriends until he met 14-year-old Dixie Locke at a church function in 1954. They dated for around two years and 19-year-old Elvis attended her junior prom at South Side High School in 1954. They were genuinely close, confided in one another, and planned to marry. They spent days together at each other's homes, went to the movies, and hung out together. Gladys approved, wanting nothing better than for her son to settle down and start a family. It was a typical teenage romance.

Dixie witnessed Elvis' career progress right from the start. As Elvis grew more famous and increasingly caught up in a new world of late nights and touring, Dixie saw less and less of him. They eventually grew apart and their relationship ended.

In 1955 she met and married another man—Elvis can't have been surprised.

The last time Dixie saw Elvis was at his mother's funeral in August 1958 at Graceland.

LEFT *Elvis and Dixie Locke on her prom night, 1954.*

1949–1956
AN OVERNIGHT SENSATION

SUN STUDIOS

"I don't sound like nobody."

ELVIS PRESLEY TO MARION KEISKER, 1953

Sometime in the summer of 1953, after Elvis had graduated from high school, he walked into the Sun Studios on Union Avenue, Memphis, to cut a demo, ostensibly as a birthday present for his mother. He had to pay around $4 to record "My Happiness" and "That's Where Your Heartaches Begin". Studio manager and producer Sam Phillips wasn't there, but his assistant Marion Keisker was. When she asked Elvis what he sounded like, he famously replied, "I don't sound like nobody." Something about Elvis impressed her. She took his name, recorded him (something she didn't normally do), and said she'd mention him to her boss.

Phillips never called, but in January 1954, Elvis, who was working for Crown Electric as a truck driver and studying to be an electrician at night, strode back into Sun to make another demo. This time, Phillips was there and he was impressed. Here was something he'd been looking for: a white man who sounded like a black man—he could see the potential. Nevertheless, it wasn't until the summer of that year that he finally called Elvis. Phillips had found a ballad, "Without You," that he thought would suit the young singer: Would Elvis come in and record it? Phillips lined up two local musicians, Scotty Moore and Bill Black, to accompany Elvis and called them in for rehearsal. Elvis wanted to sing in the style of Dean Martin, but Sam Phillips thought he sounded terrible. The song eventually chosen was "That's All Right".

Did You Know?

Jerry Lee Lewis, Roy Orbison, and Johnny Cash all started their recording careers with Sun Studios in the 1950s.

LEFT *Elvis at home with Sam Phillips, private party 1957.*

THAT'S ALL RIGHT (MAMA)

When Elvis sang "That's All Right (Mama)" in the Sun Studios in July 1954 with Scotty Moore on lead guitar and Bill Black on bass, Sam Phillips knew he'd been right to invest studio time in the young singer. "That's All Right" (Elvis dropped the "Mama") was to be Elvis' first single, released on September 4, 1954. A success on the local Southern charts, it was the song that set Elvis on the road to stardom. Written and originally recorded by the black blues singer Arthur Crudup, the blues piece was transformed into something altogether more rock 'n' roll. Nobody had ever heard anything like it.

The recording emerged at the end of a long day in the studio, which had not produced anything usable. The story goes that a tired but ever-playful Elvis began to fool around with the song, Scotty and Bill joined in, and Sam hit the "record" button.

Two days later, the locally famous Memphis disc jockey Dewey Phillips played "That's All Right" on his Red Hot and Blue show on WHBQ. Audience response was overwhelming and later that night a nervous Presley came in for his first interview. Years later, Elvis attempted (but failed) to get Arthur Crudup the royalties he was owed for this and other songs.

Facts

★ **B-Side:** "Blue Moon of Kentucky"
★ **Released:** September 4, 1954
★ **Label:** Sun Records
★ **Writer:** Arthur Crudup
★ **Producer:** Sam Phillips
★ **Chart Success:** Did not chart nationally in the USA but did chart locally on the Southern charts.

Did You Know?

"That's All Right" was recorded as if it were being played live. The vocals and musical accompaniment were laid down at the same time on a single track.

the LOUISIANA HAYRIDE

Continuing to work as a truck driver for Crown Electric, Elvis began to tour with Scotty and Bill, playing in a variety of venues, such as school halls, clubs, and church halls, with Scotty acting as the group's manager. By October, Elvis was appearing regularly on the *Louisiana Hayride*, a live Saturday country music radio show, where he typically sang "It's All Right" and "Blue Moon of Kentucky". Weeks before his first *Hayride* performance, Elvis had appeared on the *Hayride*'s main competitor, the *Grand Ole Opry* in Nashville. His performance hadn't gone down well with the country audience and he was told by the manager that he should stick to truck driving. He was greatly upset by this (Scotty recalled him crying over it), and so the *Hayride* became incredibly important to Elvis. He was paid

$18 a night and signed a contract for 51 weeks. His good looks—gelled hair, piercing eyes (already accentuated with mascara), unique sound, and explicitly sexual moves were gaining him fame and notoriety all over the South. The critics, however, weren't impressed, commenting that he couldn't sing. But as his stage presence and confidence grew, he became capable of literally whipping up hysteria, in teenage girls in particular. Jealous boyfriends took swipes at him backstage, but he took it all in his stride. The hysteria grew rapidly, until no other artist was prepared to follow him on stage—the 19-year-old Elvis, known as the Hillbilly Cat, always closed the show.

LEFT AND OPPOSITE *Elvis with guitarist Scotty Moore and bass player Bill Black on tour with the* Louisiana Hayride, *October 1954.*

> "Some people tap their feet, some people snap their fingers, and some people sway back and forth. I just sorta do 'em all together, I guess."
>
> ELVIS, 1956

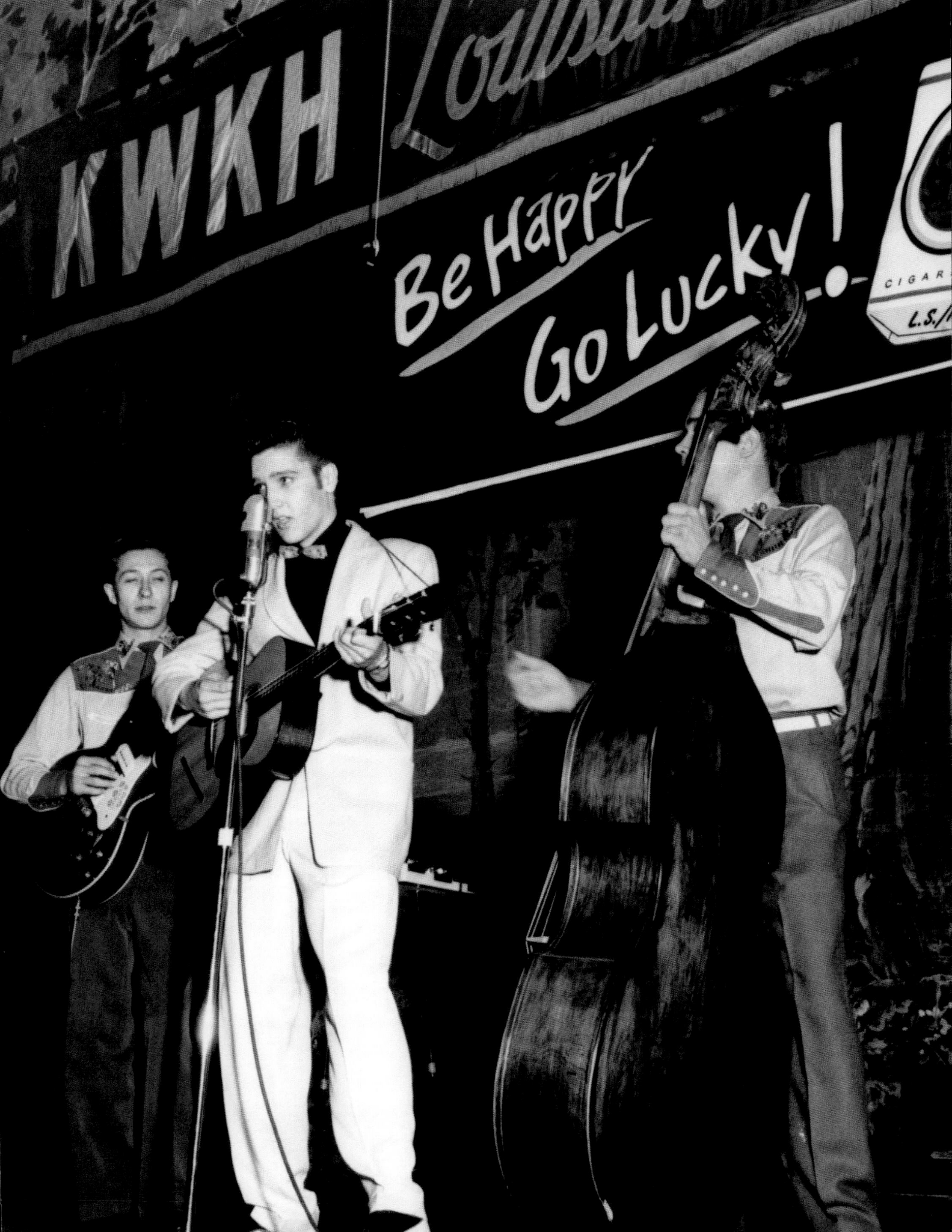
KWKH
Be Happy
Go Lucky!
CIGAR
L.S./

"Colonel"
PARKER

By the spring of 1955, Elvis had released five singles with Sun, some of which had charted nationally, and had a new manager, Bob Neal. Neal booked Elvis, Scotty, and Bill on a tour with country singer Hank Snow. The tour was organized by Hank Snow Jamboree Attractions, which was owned by Snow but operated by a former carnival barker, now a country and western promoter, "Colonel" Tom Parker. A sharp and wily operator, Parker had heard Elvis on several occasions and, recognizing his potential, was keen to get involved. He offered to help Neal with bookings and then negotiated to take over as Elvis' manager.

By the end of 1955, the Colonel had signed Elvis to RCA for the then staggering figure of $35,000—the largest amount paid for a single performer up to that time. The Colonel was to take a 25 percent share of Elvis' income. Elvis also received $5,000 in back royalties, with which he bought his mother a pink Cadillac. A major step in Elvis' career, the move to RCA meant that Elvis would soon become a nationally known artist.

RIGHT *Elvis in 1960, on the day of his discharge from the army, with Colonel Tom Parker in the background.*

Did You Know?

Colonel Parker's real name was Andreas Cornelius van Kuijk, and he was an illegal immigrant from the Netherlands, where he was born in 1909. He was given the honorary title of "Colonel" by the Governor of Louisiana for helping to raise political funds. A controversial figure, he ruthlessly exploited his protégé throughout Elvis' career, eventually taking up to 50 percent of his income.

HEARTBREAK HOTEL

By the beginning of 1956, Elvis was well known in the South and had a large and exuberant teenage following. His records sold well and his live performances attracted adoration as well as controversy. But he wasn't yet truly famous nationally. That was all to change when, on January 10, 1956, just two days after his 21st birthday, he had his first recording session for RCA. One of the first songs recorded at this Nashville session was "Heartbreak Hotel".

The origins of "Heartbreak Hotel" came from a suicide note found in a Miami hotel, which contained the words "I walk a lonely street." Songwriter Tommy Durden took the line to another songwriter, Mae Boren Axton, and she completed it with Elvis in mind. A demo was made and sent to RCA producer Steve Sholes.

Elvis, Scotty, and Bill were joined in Nashville by backing musicians, a pianist and a drummer. Sholes was unhappy with the result, but Elvis loved it. An instinctive performer, his instincts proved to be right. Just a few weeks into its release, it had sold 300,000 records. The song catapulted Elvis into stardom.

Facts

★ **B-Side:** "I Was The One"
★ **Released:** January 27, 1956
★ **Label:** RCA
★ **Writer:** Mae Boren Axton and Thomas Durden
★ **Producer:** Steve Sholes
★ **Chart Success:** No. 1 on Billboard's pop chart; No. 1 on the Country chart; No. 5 on the R&B charts.

Did You Know?

"Heartbreak Hotel" sold over one million copies and earned Elvis a gold record award.

RIGHT *Elvis holding his gold record award for "Heartbreak Hotel", April 1956.*

OPPOSITE *Elvis recording in a studio for RCA, January 1956.*

LEFT *Elvis performing on the Milton Berle Show, June 5, 1956.*

a TV STAR IS BORN

"The brash, loud braying of his rhythm and blues catalog ... which albeit rocketed him to the big time, is overbearing to a captive audience. In a lounge, one can up and go—fast. But in a dining room, the table sitter must stay, look, and listen the thing out."

BILL WILLARD, *LAS VEGAS SUN*, APRIL 25, 1956

On January 28, 1956, Elvis appeared for the first time on national television on the *Tommy and Jimmy Dorsey Stage Show*. He made five subsequent appearances, although he was also was still appearing on the *Louisiana Hayride*. The Colonel then booked him for two appearances on the *Milton Berle Show* on ABC. Milton Berle was a popular television personality and comedian in the 1950s, known as "Mr Television." For Elvis to appear on the show was a coup for the Colonel. Elvis' first appearance on the *Milton Berle Show* was on April 5, on a show that was, rather bizarrely, broadcast from the deck of an aircraft carrier. Elvis sang "Heartbreak Hotel" and "Blue Suede Shoes". For his second appearance in June, he sang "Hound Dog" for the first time, doing two versions on the one show. The first was at the usual tempo, with his by now familiar gyrations, then he slid into a slower version, during which his movements became slower and more pronounced. The audience went wild; the press the next day were condemnatory. Uniting with religious leaders, they pronounced that Elvis was obscene. Elvis tried to defend himself in a subsequent interview. The moves, he explained, were just natural to him—they were never meant to be vulgar. But by now Elvis was a star.

ABOVE *Rehearsing for the* Milton Berle Show, *June 4, 1956.*

Milton Berle Show

Elvis Presley rehearses for his performance on the *Milton Berle Show* on June 4, 1956, with the Jordanaires, his backing group, in Burbank, California. It was at this time that his dance moves first outraged conservative audiences across the United States (see below), but his teenage fans loved it.

A group crowd around him as he takes a break during rehearsals (see right).

The main picture shows Elvis and other cast members as they rehearse a musical number.

the STEVE ALLEN SHOW

"We want to do a show that the whole family can enjoy."

STEVE ALLEN,
INTRODUCING THE SHOW

On July 1, 1956, Elvis appeared on the *Steve Allen Show*. The censors were nervous of Elvis after the *Milton Berle Show* performance. Though the TV network wanted this Elvis—they knew the ratings would be great—they didn't want the controversy. How much of the resulting solution was due to Steve Allen's dislike of rock 'n' roll (he was a jazz man) or the network's nervousness isn't clear. Elvis was dressed in a tuxedo and set up to sing "Hound Dog" comedically to a Basset hound. He played along gallantly, but looked uncomfortable, occasionally cupping the dog's face and singing directly to it. His performance was restrained; his fans were furious.

The next TV performance lined up by the Colonel was for Steve Allen's rival, Ed Sullivan. Elvis' fee of $50,000 for three shows was the highest ever paid to an artist at that time. Sullivan had said that he wouldn't have Elvis on his show, but rivalry with Allen led to a change of mind, if not heart. Elvis' first appearance was on September 9, 1956. Because of worries about the censors, for some of the show Elvis is shown from the waist up. He sang "Don't be Cruel", "Love Me Tender", "Ready Teddy", and "Hound Dog". The ratings were the highest ever for any TV show. Elvis was on a roll. In August, he had started filming his first movie, *Love Me Tender*.

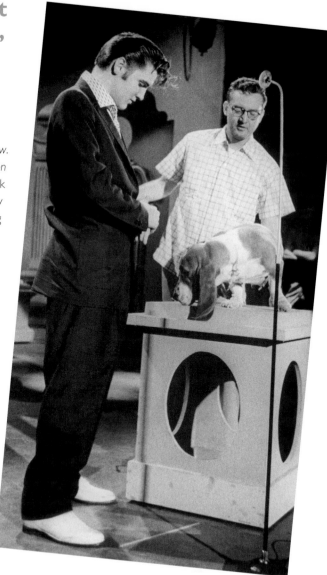

OPPOSITE *Rehearsing for the* Steve Allen Show, *June 29, 1956.*

ABOVE *Singing "Hound Dog" for Steve Allen and a Bassett hound during a rehearsal.*

the JORDANAIRES

E lvis first approached the Jordanaires in October 1954, after hearing them at the Ellis Auditorium in Memphis. At the time, Elvis was still signed to Sun. The Jordanaires were a white quartet, founded by two evangelists, who sang gospel, Elvis' first love. Elvis was just beginning his career when he approached them backstage, saying, "If I ever get a recording contract with a major company, I want you guys to back me up." Once he was signed to RCA, he kept his promise. In 1956, the Jordanaires started backing him and continued to do so until 1969. They featured on 28 of his movie soundtracks and on hits such as "Are You Lonesome Tonight?" and "Jailhouse Rock". They joined Elvis for one of his earliest recordings for RCA, on July 2, 1956, in New York, when they recorded "Hound Dog" and "Don't be Cruel". Elvis insisted that the Jordanaires be credited on the record labels, which was not the usual practice for backing artists at that time. The members of the Jordanaires between 1954 and 1956 were Hoyt Hawkins, Gordon Stoker, Neal Matthews, and Hugh Jarrett. Ray Walker replaced Jarrett in 1958. Over the years there have been 16 members and they are still going strong today.

LEFT *Performing with his backing group, the Jordanaires, January 1956.*

Elvis Presley
THE ALBUM

On March 13, 1956, *Elvis Presley* was released. The album had been recorded in January in Nashville and New York, with the addition of some earlier Sun Studios material. Bill, Scotty, the by-now regular drummer DJ Fontana, and the Jordanaires performed on it. A mix of country and rhythm and blues tracks, it was quintessential Elvis. *Rolling Stone* magazine made it No. 55 in their top 500 albums of all time. In 2006, Sony BMG reissued the album.

The album went to number one on Billboard's pop album chart in 1956, where it remained for ten weeks. It was Elvis' first album to reach over $1 million in sales and earned him his first gold album award.

While Elvis topped the album charts, on April 1 his career took a new turn when he did a successful screen test with Paramount Pictures and signed a seven-year contract.

Did You Know?

Carl Perkins wrote the album's first track "Blue Suede Shoes".

ABOVE *Musician Steve Sholes talking to producer Chet Atkins while Elvis rests during an RCA recording session, April 1956.*

OPPOSITE *Singing and playing piano during an RCA recording session, September 1956.*

The Album Tracks

★ **Side 1**
★ "Blue Suede Shoes"
★ "I'm Counting on You"
★ "I Got A Woman"
★ "One-Sided Love Affair"
★ "I Love You Because"
★ "Just Because"

Side 2
★ "Tutti Frutti"
★ "Trying To Get You"
★ "I'm Gonna Sit Down and Cry (Over You)"
★ "I'll Never Let You Go (Lil' Darlin')"
★ "Blue Moon"
★ "Money Honey"

DON'T BE CRUEL

Originally "Don't Be Cruel" was the A-side of the RCA single, with "Hound Dog" on the B-side, although they were later released as a double A-side, and both went to No. 1 on the United States Billboard charts. "Don't Be Cruel" was the first to top all three Billboard charts: pop, R&B, and country and western.

The song was recorded for RCA Victor by Elvis' regular band of Scotty on lead guitar, Bill on bass, and DJ Fontana on drums, with backing vocals from the Jordanaires. Elvis recorded it on July 2 at RCA's New York City studio—it took him somewhere between 12 and 23 takes to get it right. Elvis reworked the music and lyrics and earned himself a songwriting credit on the label. "Don't Be Cruel" is No. 197 in *Rolling Stone*'s list of the 500 Greatest Songs of all Time.

ELVIS AND OTIS

Otis Blackwell was a brilliant singer-songwriter who wrote several hits for Elvis, including "All Shook Up" and "Return to Sender". He wrote "Great Balls of Fire" for Jerry Lee Lewis and "Fever", a big hit for Peggy Lee. Otis Blackwell grew up listening to R&B and country music and, although he and Elvis had, in effect, a musical collaboration lasting several years, they never actually met. Blackwell died in 2002 at the age of 70.

OPPOSITE *Elvis
performing "Hound
Dog" live, August 1956.*

Facts

★ **B-Side:** "Hound Dog"
★ **Released:** July 13, 1956
★ **Label:** RCA
★ **Writer:** Otis Blackwell
★ **Producer:** Steve Sholes
★ **Chart Success:** No. 1 on Billboard's
   Country & Western, R&B, and Pop charts.

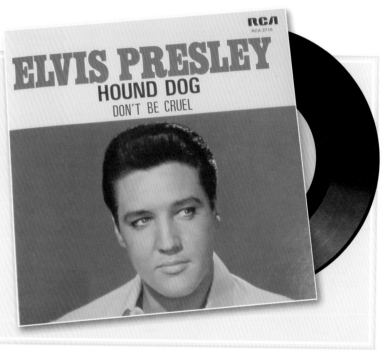

ELVIS PRESLEY DAY

In August 1956, Elvis began shooting his first movie, *Love Me Tender* (page 58). He was still touring and recording and now he was filming. On September 26, 1956, Elvis Presley Day was proclaimed in his hometown of Tupelo. Banners were stretched across Main Street as busloads of teenage girls arrived. Elvis had been invited to perform two shows at the Mississippi–Alabama Fair and Dairy Show, where, at the age of ten, he had won a prize for singing "Old Shep".

One hundred national guardsmen were brought in to control the thousands of mostly female fans. His relationship with his fans was pretty much set by that time: they adored him and he would always acknowledge them, taking the time to sign autographs, chat, and joke. Both he and his parents gave interviews and Elvis later donated his fee for the performances to the city of Tupelo.

Later in October Elvis made a second appearance on Ed Sullivan. He performed "Don't Be Cruel", "Love Me Tender", "Love Me", and a four-minute-long version of "Hound Dog"—this time he was shown in full throughout the song. During the show, Ed Sullivan remarked that he just didn't understand the Elvis thing.

ELVIS MERCHANDISE

By 1957, Elvis souvenirs were available—the beginning of a merchandising trade that the Colonel had launched and which is still big today. Aimed at the teenage girl fan base, there were Elvis statues, clothing, postcards, scent, stationery, and much more.

RIGHT *Performing in Tupelo, Mississippi on a day in his honor, September 1956.*

1957–1958
SUPERSTARDOM

HOLLYWOOD CALLS

"He can sing but he can't do much else."

NATALIE WOOD

Elvis had signed a contract with Paramount Pictures in April 1956. By August 1956, he was in Hollywood filming his first movie, *Love Me Tender*. By all accounts, Elvis was excited and eager to get to Hollywood. In interviews, he talked about his ambition to get better at acting. He identified with James Dean and thought that maybe he could be as good as he had been one day. Elvis would not have realized at this time that he would spend the next 13 years making 31 movies in Hollywood and that he would never reach his own aim of becoming a serious actor. In all but one of his movies, he was required to sing, something he had not really set out to do.

Right from the beginning, however, there was plenty of fun, and Elvis made a habit of dating his leading ladies and actresses. In 1956, he was introduced to the actress Natalie Wood, who had starred in *Rebel Without A Cause* with one of Elvis' heroes, James Dean.

NATALIE'S VISIT

Although Elvis was dating another girl at that time, a Biloxi beauty queen named Juan Juanica, he invited Natalie Wood to stay with him and his parents in Memphis during a break from filming. The visit went badly: Elvis introduced Natalie to the sights of Memphis, took her pillion on his motorcycle, but Natalie found life with Gladys and Vernon overbearing and Elvis, apparently, a little dull. She left after only four days and, reputedly, said of Elvis that 'He can sing but he can't do much else.'' The visit also led to the end of Elvis' more serious relationship with Juan Juanica.

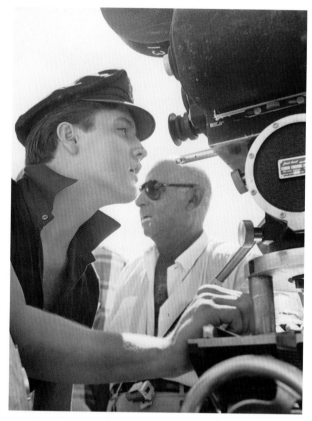

ABOVE *Elvis takes an interest in the camera on the set of* Girls, Girls, Girls *1963.*

OPPOSITE *Elvis with Natalie Wood, November 1956.*

LOVE ME TENDER
The movie

Love Me Tender was directed by Robert Webb and released in November 1956 by Twentieth Century Fox, who had Elvis on loan from Paramount. The movie premiered in New York at the Paramount Theater. A western, it starred Robert Egan and Debra Paget, with Elvis in a secondary role, the only time in his movie career that this happened.

Elvis played Clint Reno, whose brothers leave home to fight for the Confederates in the Civil War. When news arrives that one brother, Vance, has been killed on the battlefield, Clint marries Vance's fiancée, Cathy. However, Vance returns and the situation is resolved by a gunfight between Clint and Vance, ending with Clint's murder. Elvis fans were so distraught by the leaked news that Elvis' character dies at the end of the movie that the producer was forced to alter the ending. In the final movie, a ghostly Elvis rises from death, playing the title song on his guitar. Time would prove Love Me Tender to be atypical of Elvis' movies—not only does he die; he sings only four songs.

Although the movie was number eight in the top ten grossing movies of 1956, it received poor reviews, with Time magazine comparing Elvis' acting ability to a "Walt Disney Goldfish."

ELVIS' CRUSH

During filming, Elvis developed a crush on his co-star, Debra Paget, an established and beautiful actress, whom he had previously met on the Milton Berle Show. She, however, didn't return his feelings. Many have since commented on how similar Debra's looks were to th

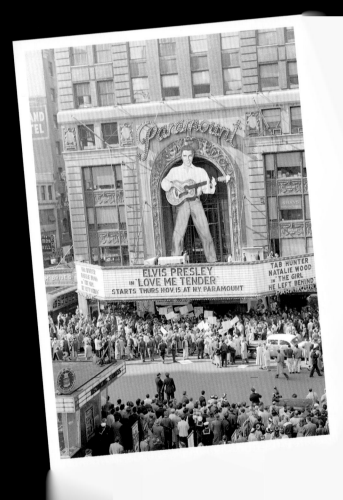

The music

Recorded on the sound stage at Twentieth Century Fox on August 24, 1956, the single "Love Me Tender" was released that September. Elvis had popularized the ballad on September 9 on the *Ed Sullivan Show*. After the show, RCA received requests for one million advance copies.

Much to RCA's chagrin, the movie's producer decided not to use Elvis' regular band on the soundtrack. Instead, the Ken Darby Trio, who had backed Bing Crosby on "White Christmas", would provide the musical backing. The song was written by Ken Darby, an award-winning composer, but for royalty reasons his wife, Vera Matson, was credited, along with Elvis. Although Elvis certainly didn't co-write the song, he was very involved in its production. The music was taken from "Aura Lee", a popular and sentimental Civil War ballad that Darby had reworked.

RIGHT *Elvis rehearsing "Love Me Tender" for The Ed Sullivan Show, September 9, 1956.*

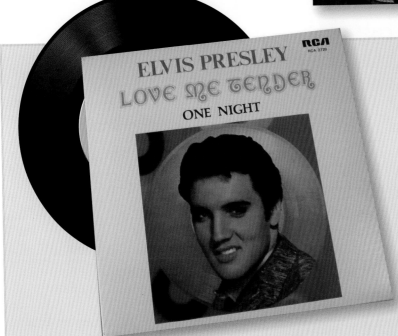

Chart Position

The single "Love Me Tender" was No. 1 for five weeks on the Billboard pop singles chart. There was no album for the movie, but its four songs were released on an EP (extended play) 45. It went to No. 9 on the pop album chart in the USA.

ALL SHOOK UP

Elvis recorded "All Shook Up" at the RCA Studios in Hollywood, just before he started shooting his second movie, *Loving You*. The recording session went smoothly and Elvis personally liked the song. It became a hit, the second written by Otis Blackwell, who had also penned "Don't Be Cruel". Blackwell apparently wrote "All Shook Up" after he was dared to include the words "All Shook Up" in a song by a friend, who had just shaken a bottle of Pepsi. Blackwell obliged and produced what was to become Billboard's song of 1957. "All Shook Up" was the song that introduced the classic "uh-huh-huh" to the Presley repertoire.

Just before recording the single, Elvis had made his third and final appearance on the *Ed Sullivan Show*. Ironically, given all the controversy about his hip shaking, one of the songs that Elvis sang on that occasion was the soulful gospel song, "Peace in the Valley".

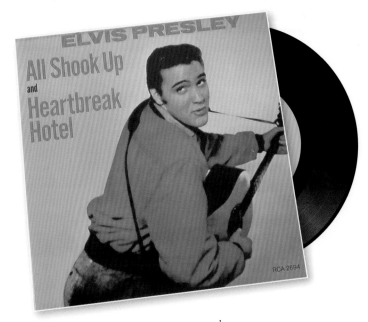

Facts

★ **B-Side:** "That's Where Your Heartaches Begin"
★ **Released:** March 22, 1957
★ **Recorded:** January 12, 1957
★ **Label:** RCA
★ **Writer:** Otis Blackwell
★ **Producer:** Steve Sholes
★ **Chart Success:** It reached the top of all three US charts (pop, country, and R&B), staying there for eight weeks in 1957, from April 13 through May 27.

Did You Know?

"All Shook Up" stayed on Billboard's Pop chart for 30 weeks—this was the longest stay on any chart of any Elvis single.

OPPOSITE *Performing on the* Ed Sullivan Show *for the last time, January 6, 1957.*

At home in
GRACELAND

From 1956 until 1957, Elvis and his family lived in Audubon Drive in Memphis. However, it soon became apparent, after complaints from local residents, that the hullaballoo Elvis caused meant he needed a more secure and private home. In March 1957, Elvis bought Graceland for himself and his parents, fulfilling his boyhood dream of providing for them and giving them a good home.

Bought for $100,000, Graceland was a white colonnaded building. Its address was 3764 Elvis Presley Boulevard (formerly South Bellevue Road). A 500-acre (200-ha) farm from the era of the American Civil War, Graceland had around 23 rooms and stood on nearly 14 acres (6 ha). His mother immediately added a chicken coop to remind her of country life in Tupelo. Elvis was to live there until his death, as was his paternal grandmother, Minnie Mae Presley, who outlived Elvis, Vernon, and Gladys.

Though he spent much time away touring and filming, Graceland was the place Elvis considered home. Graceland became his refuge. Here, he felt safe from the crowds of adoring fans whom he loved, but whom he could keep at the famous gates. Secure on the other side, Elvis would wave at and even talk to them.

It was a long way from the two-room shotgun shack of his birth.

The Name Graceland

The origin of the name Graceland is unclear, though it is thought to have been named after Grace Toof, the daughter of its original owner, publisher SE Toof.

RIGHT *Elvis stands at the colonnaded entrance to Graceland in March 1957.*

OPPOSITE *Elvis enjoys a walk on the lawns of his new mansion in 1957.*

LOVING YOU

Elvis started shooting *Loving You* in January 1957 at the Paramount Studios in Hollywood. The movie, written by Hal Kanter and produced by Hal Wallis (who produced nine of Elvis' movies), was created as a vehicle especially for Elvis. Shot in glorious Technicolor, it was much more suited to Elvis than *Love Me Tender*. The main character, Deke Rivers, was pretty much autobiographical, and the story depicted the rise of a truck driver to singing superstardom. There was even a Colonel Parker-type character, played by Lizabeth Scott—a female manager who tries to exploit her protégé.

The song "Teddy Bear" and the final sequence in which Elvis sings "Got A Lot o' Livin' To Do" were Elvis at his best. "Teddy Bear" went to No. 1 in the Billboard pop chart. The film is also noted for Elvis' first screen kiss. The actress Jana Lund, who plays Daisy Bricker, steals a kiss from Elvis' character as part of a dare. Gladys and Vernon Presley even appear in the audience while Elvis performs "Got a Lot o' Livin' to Do". After his mother's death, Elvis was never able to view the movie again.

Loving You premiered in Memphis on July 9, 1957, at the Strand Theater and opened nationally on July 30. It reached No. 7 on *Variety*'s weekly top-grossing movie list, although the critics didn't like it. Elvis didn't go to the premiere but instead took his girlfriend Anita Wood and his parents to a private midnight screening. In later years, when Elvis felt his fame prevented him from attending the cinema along with the general public, he came to view all his films at private night-time screenings.

Did You Know?

Inspired by Tony Curtis, Elvis dyed his hair black for the role of Deke Rivers. His hair was naturally light brown and Elvis believed he would look more striking on celluloid with black hair. He liked it so much he kept his hair black from then on, only reverting to his natural colour when he served as a GI.

RIGHT *Elvis on a motorcycle with* Loving You *co-star Yvonne Lime, 1957.*

OPPOSITE *Playing guitar for the movie* Loving You, *1957.*

JAILHOUSE ROCK The movie

Filmed in black and white by MGM, *Jailhouse Rock* was released in Memphis on October 15, 1957 and nationally on November 8, 1957. Despite poor reviews, it is today considered one of Elvis' best movies, with the titular song and dance number now a classic Elvis moment. Filming began in May and finished in June, after which Elvis returned to Memphis, staying at Graceland for the first time.

Elvis plays Vince Everett, who is sent to jail after being convicted of manslaughter following a bar brawl over a girl, which he didn't start. In jail, he is taught the guitar by another inmate, Hunk Houghton, a washed-up country singer, who recognizes that Vince has talent. When Vince is released, he tries to get work as a singer and meets up with Peggy van Alden (played by Judy Tyler), a record promoter. Eventually, after a series of failures,

Vince finds his own voice and style of music and, very much as had happened to Elvis in real life, becomes a star. The success goes to Vince's head, and it takes a serious voice-threatening injury caused by a fight with Hunk to bring him to his senses. The movie's highlight, the "Jailhouse Rock" sequence, was partly choreographed by Elvis himself.

Tragically, Elvis' co-star and love interest, newlywed Judy Tyler, was killed with her husband just a few weeks after the completion of filming. Elvis was devastated when he heard the news, and was never able to watch the completed movie.

Despite the by now usual panning by the critics, *Jailhouse Rock* reached No. 3 in *Variety*'s weekly list, and No. 14 in *Variety*'s list of annual top-grossing movies. One critic even described the movie as "dreadful," "nauseating," and "queasy-making."

The music

The soundtrack for *Jailhouse Rock* was recorded in Hollywood, with Scotty, Bill, DJ Fontana, and the Jordanaires, and was released as an EP in October 1957. The record included "Young and Beautiful", "I Want to be Free", "Don't Leave Me Now", "(You're So Square) Baby I Don't Care", and, of course, "Jailhouse Rock". The latter has been named as one of the rock 'n' roll Hall of Fame's 500 songs that shaped Rock 'n' Roll. Released as a single in September to coincide with the movie's release, it went to No. 1 on Billboard's pop chart in the United States for seven weeks. In October, the EP reached No. 1 in the United States. It topped the Billboard EP charts, eventually going double platinum and selling more than four million records.

Written by Jerry Leiber and Mike Stoller, the performance of the title song is considered one of Elvis' finest screen moments. Full of raw energy, it capitalized on Elvis' youth and vitality and many music critics believe that this was the moment when rock 'n' roll became integrated into American culture and society.

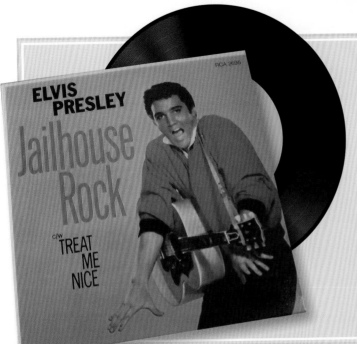

Leiber and Stoller

A highly successful songwriting duo, Mike Leiber and Jerry Stoller wrote several of Elvis' hits, including "Hound Dog", "Loving You", and "Jailhouse Rock". Other hits included The Drifters' "There Goes My Baby" and "Yakety Yak" for the Coasters.

ABOVE *Elvis with Mike Stoller and Jerry Leiber looking over "Jailhouse Rock" sheet music, 1957.*

OPPOSITE *Elvis in a dance scene from the movie.*

the MILLION DOLLAR Quartet

In December 1957, an impromptu jamming session took place at the Sun Studios; it became known as the Million Dollar Quartet. Carl Perkins (who had already recorded "Blue Suede Shoes"), Jerry Lee Lewis (who was relatively unknown), Johnny Cash, and Elvis Presley made up the quartet. They all found themselves at the studio just before Christmas by chance. Elvis had just popped in to say hello to Sam. They started jamming, with Elvis at the piano, and each taking turns with lead vocal (although Cash's voice cannot really be heard). There is a lot of chatter and laughter and the songs reflect the singers themselves, with country and gospel being prominent, although there is an eclectic mix with "White Christmas", "Jingle Bells", "I Shall Not Be Moved", "When The Saints Go Marching In", and "Brown-Eyed Handsome Man", among many others. All are sung with great spontaneity. Elvis also sings a soulful "Peace in the Valley", a song he would later record with great success.

Sam Phillips had the forethought to record some of the session. He also called the local paper, the *Memphis Press Scimitar*, who sent a reporter and photographer, and the session became known as the Million Dollar Quartet. The tapes weren't released for more than 20 years, but are available today.

A YOUTHFUL QUARTET

They may have been worth a million dollars, but they were still very young. Elvis and Lewis were both 21 years old, while Cash and Perkins were old timers at 24.

LEFT *Elvis with Johnny Cash, taken in December 1957.*

OPPOSITE *Elvis playing piano and singing with Jerry Lee Lewis, Carl Perkins, and Johnny Cash, December 4, 1956.*

1957–1960
THE DRAFT &
PRISCILLA

the *the* DRAFT

"It's a duty I've got to fulfill and I'm going to do it."

ELVIS

On December 10, 1957, Elvis received a letter from the Memphis Draft Board notifying him that he was soon to be drafted into the military. At this time in the United States all able-bodied men were required to do two years' military service and Elvis would have been expecting the draft, although he had also planned to start filming his fourth movie, *King Creole*, in January. On December 20, 1957, Elvis picked up his draft notice in person. He was to report for induction into the army on January 20, 1958.

Hal Wallis, the producer of *King Creole*, and Paramount Pictures were desperate not to lose their star—without Elvis the movie would most certainly have been canceled, although $350,000 had already been spent on it. Elvis himself was worried that a two-year gap would end his movie career.

Colonel Parker and Paramount wrote to the Memphis Draft Board, asking that Elvis' draft be deferred until late March. Their request mirrored the feelings of thousands of angry fans who wanted their King at home. The Draft Board agreed to grant Elvis a 60-day deferment.

Elvis was offered special duties by both the army and the navy, but he rejected these, saying he wanted to be a GI just like anyone else.

OPPOSITE *In uniform during basic training at Fort Hood, Texas, March, 1958.*

LEFT *Being sworn into the US Army in 1958.*

KING CREOLE

"Elvis Presley can act ... Acting is his assignment in this shrewdly upholstered showcase, and he does it."

HOWARD THOMPSON, THE *NEW YORK TIMES*, 1958

A high-quality cast and production team was assembled for *King Creole*. It was directed by Michael Curtiz, who had directed *Casablanca* and *Yankee Doodle Dandy*, and produced by Hal Wallis. The story was based on Harold Robbins' novel *A Stone for Danny Fisher*. Production began on January 20, 1958, and finished on March 10—just a few days before Elvis was to report to the army.

In the movie, Elvis plays Danny Fisher, a young man born in the New Orleans ghetto, who seeks fame and fortune as a singer in the New Orleans jazz clubs. Along the way he encounters gangland boss Maxie Fields, played by Walter Matthau, and his moll Ronnie (Elvis' love interest), played by Carolyn Jones (who later found fame as Morticia in the American television series *The Addams Family*).

Elvis stayed in New Orleans for the filming. Besieged by fans, he was unable to walk about the city freely or to eat in restaurants, and most nights he was alone in his hotel room. It was the beginning of a habit of isolation and seclusion, which became more ingrained as his life progressed.

The movie was released on July 2, 1958, by which time Elvis was in Germany. Despite lukewarm reviews, it was ranked by *Variety* as the ninth top-grossing movie of 1958.

KING CREOLE CHART SUCCESS
On July 21, the *King Creole* soundtrack entered Billboards pop chart, peaking at No. 2.

LEFT *Recording the soundtrack for the movie* King Creole, *1958.*

the US ARMY

On March 25, Elvis reported to the Memphis Draft Board, accompanied by his parents, his girlfriend Anita Wood, and other friends, as well as hordes of fans and photographers. The army had never seen anything like it. Elvis was sworn in as Private Presley 53310761 and then left on an army bus for Fort Chaffee, Arkansas, for basic training. His mother, father, and Anita were all in tears. In fact, Gladys was distraught, unaware that Elvis would soon be living off base with his family.

At Fort Chafee, Elvis received his famous GI haircut—he retained his natural hair shade for the duration of his army career. He was assigned to the Second Armored Division, stationed at Fort Hood, Texas. He seems to have tolerated army life, making friends and generally making the most of it. Although homesick (he called his mother every day), he had earned a marksman's medal by May and had become acting assistant leader of his squad.

In June, he received two weeks' leave and returned to Graceland. RCA arranged a recording session in Nashville, which would give the Colonel more material to release during Elvis' absence. The session was Elvis' last before his discharge in 1960.

On his return to Fort Hood, Elvis was given the standard soldier's permission to live off base with his "dependants." This meant his mother, father, paternal grandmother, and various friends who were not really his "dependants," but he got away with it. He rented a nearby house for extended family. His mother was happy. For the time being, life in the army seemed just about OK.

RIGHT *The Presley family seeing Elvis off at the bus station as he leaves for Fort Chaffee. His mother is the woman crying in the front of the crowd, March 26, 1958.*

Elvis' MOTHER DIES

> **"Not mine but thy will be done."**
>
> INSCRIPTION ON THE TOMB OF
> GLADYS PRESLEY

In July 1958, Elvis was living in a rented house near Fort Hood with his parents and other members of his family. Gladys' health had been affected by Elvis' fame: the persistence of the fans, who often tore his clothes; the death threats; the hatred he engendered in certain sections of society; and his induction into the army caused her enormous stress and suffering. She had started to take diet pills and was drinking heavily.

By August, Elvis and Vernon were so concerned that they persuaded her to return to Memphis to see Elvis' personal physician. A day later, Gladys was taken by ambulance to hospital in Memphis. A desperate Elvis was granted leave to visit his by now gravely ill mother. He spent many hours by her hospital bedside with his father and then returned home to Graceland, where, at quarter past three in the morning on August 14, he received a call from his father: Gladys had passed away. She had died of acute hepatitis and heart failure at the age of 46.

Elvis was distraught and wept inconsolably at the funeral. Friends and close associates say he was never the same again. At the funeral, he was heard to say, "Everything I have is gone."

Gladys was buried in the Forest Hill Cemetery near Graceland. Elvis had inscribed the text "Not mine but thy will be done" on her tomb. After Elvis' death, both he and his mother were interred at Graceland.

LEFT *Elvis with his parents, Vernon and Gladys, 1958.*

"Everything I have is gone."

ELVIS, AT HIS MOTHER'S FUNERAL

"I hope I can live up to everyone's
expectations of me."

ELVIS, ON HIS ARRIVAL IN GERMANY

Elvis arrives in
GERMANY

On August 24, Elvis returned to Fort Hood and was assigned to the Third Armored Division. On September 19, still raw from his mother's funeral, he went by train to New York with 1,400 members of his company to board a ship bound for West Germany. When he arrived in New York, he was met by the usual throng of reporters, photographers, and fans and was immediately asked to take part in a press conference. When Elvis was asked what kind of girl he'd like to marry, he replied, "The female kind, sir." An army band played "Hound Dog" and "All Shook Up".

On September 22, Elvis left the Brooklyn Navy Yards on board the USS *General Randall*, headed for Bremerhaven, West Germany, where he would see out the remainder of his enlistment. On October 1, the *General Randall* arrived in Bremerhaven, where, to Elvis' surprise—he had no idea he was popular in Germany—he was greeted by 2,000 screaming German fans. Before he could begin his life as an ordinary GI, he had to give yet another press conference, this time dressed in uniform. He expressed pleasure at being in Europe and said, with typical modesty, "I hope I can live up to everyone's expectations of me."

Once in Germany, he was reunited with his father and paternal grandmother Minnie Mae. For a while, the Presleys lived in hotels but later they set up house in Bad Nauheim, close to the base. They were joined by Elvis' old school friends Red West and Lamar Fike—both were later to become core members of the so-called Memphis Mafia. Elvis would eat breakfast cooked by his grandmother and even return home for lunch. Fans would gather outside the house and Elvis, true to form, would sign autographs for them.

LEFT *Elvis on board a train as he arrives in Frankfurt, Germany, October 1, 1958.*

just an ORDINARY GI

Elvis was never just an ordinary GI, although he may have appeared to be. He received hundreds of fan letters every day, and whenever he was off base, he was besieged by German fans requesting autographs. In addition, living off base meant that he could party with his friends all night. It was at this time that he was introduced to amphetamines.

Elvis was told—and believed—they were harmless; they helped him to keep up his lifestyle and still get back to base on time. It was also in the army that he learned karate, which would later become one of his real passions. In January 1959, Elvis celebrated his 24th birthday in Germany.

Elvis served in Company C, which was a scout platoon. His job was to drive a jeep, and like any other soldier in the army, he went on field exercises. By the end of his stay in 1960, he had impressed those in authority enough for him to be promoted to sergeant.

THE TRIP TO PARIS

One leave in June 1959, Elvis organized a trip to Paris, principally to try to have a meeting with the French actress Brigitte Bardot. She didn't respond to Elvis' invitation, but Elvis made sure that he and his army buddies and old friends had a great time. The group flew a chartered plane to Paris. They visited the Louvre and the Eiffel Tower and partied at various nightclubs, including the Lido nightclub, the Moulin Rouge, and the 4 O'Clock Club. The days were spent sleeping—it was the beginning of a pattern of sleeping during the day and working and partying at night that Elvis would continue for the rest of his life.

BELOW *Elvis cleaning a sign at his US military base, October 1958.*

OPPOSITE *Reading a letter while serving in Germany, 1958–1959.*

"The Girl Elvis Left Behind."

ELVIS &
PRISCILLA *meet*

Elvis met Priscilla Anne Beaulieu in November 1959 at a party in Wiesbaden, Germany. She was the 14-year-old stepdaughter of a US air force captain and an Elvis Presley fan. Her biological father, a US air force pilot, had been killed in a plane crash when she was an infant and, until her teens, she was led to believe that her stepfather was her real father.

She was wearing a blue sailor's dress when she first met Elvis at his home in Bad Nauheim. They were introduced to him by a mutual friend. He was immediately struck by her petite but striking looks—blue eyes, small turned-up nose, and fine bone structure. It seems to have been love at first sight for both. Even though Elvis had many girls in his life at this time, and a serious girlfriend at home, he seemed quite taken with by Priscilla.

Little was made of their romance by the press until photographers captured Priscilla tearfully waving goodbye to Elvis (now a sergeant) on March 1 as he boarded the plane at Frankfurt airport to leave Germany and the army and return home to Graceland and his career. She immediately became known as "The Girl Elvis Left Behind."

Once back in the United States, despite many whisperings about his romances, it became clear to friends that Elvis didn't want to be without Priscilla. He soon called for her to join him at Graceland; his father and new stepmother (Vernon had married Dee Stanley, the ex-wife of an army officer, in July 1960) would act as chaperones. Her parents agreed and, in the summer of 1962, Priscilla joined Elvis at Graceland.

OPPOSITE *Priscilla poses, pen in hand beside a photograph of Elvis*

RIGHT *Priscilla among fans, waves goodbye to Elvis as he leaves Germany at the end of his tour of duty 1960*

1960–1961
THE KING
IS BACK

ELVIS COMES HOME

When Elvis returned to the United States in March 1960, he wasn't sure what the future had in store for him. During his army years, the Colonel and RCA had released songs to keep him in the charts and in the public eye. However, there was no need to worry. From the moment Elvis stepped off the plane in New Jersey, his old life returned with a hectic schedule of planned interviews and recordings and a TV show and movie in the pipeline. One of his first tasks, however, was to visit his mother's grave to see her new memorial stone. On March 20, Elvis left Graceland for Nashville to start recording material for his next album, *Elvis Is Back*. Elvis not only sang the songs, he also produced this album.

It was a real test for Elvis and he passed with distinction. The music scene had changed since 1958 and the raw rock 'n' roll that Elvis had personified had been replaced by a smoother sixties sound. The Colonel made sure that Elvis followed this fashion. John Lennon once said that the music died when Elvis joined the army but, in most critics' view, the music simply changed. *Elvis is Back*, released on April 8, 1960, peaked at No. 2 in the pop charts. It is considered one of his finest albums—an eclectic mix of pop, blues, gospel, and rock—and it really showed Elvis' versatility, far more so than his pre-army records.

Tracks included "Fever", "The Girl of My Best Friend", and "Reconsider Baby". For the first time, Bill Black didn't play the bass on the album, although Scotty, DJ Fontana, and the Jordanaires all took part.

ABOVE *Newly released from the US Army, Elvis is surrounded by his friends in hospital, where he had received treatment for a finger injured while playing sport.*

OPPOSITE *In March 1960, Elvis arrives in New Jersey at the end of his army career.*

The Album Tracks

Side 1
★ "Make Me Know It"
★ "Fever"
★ "The Girl of My Best Friend"
★ "I Will Be Home Again"
★ "Dirty Dirty Feeling"
★ "Thrill of Your Love"

Side 2
★ "Soldier Boy"
★ "Such a Night"
★ "It Feels So Right"
★ "Girl Next Door Went a Walking"
★ "Like a Baby"
★ "Reconsider Baby"

RIGHT *Frank Sinatra and Elvis rehearse together for The Frank Sinatra Timex Show, May 1960.*

OPPOSITE *Nancy Sinatra gives Elvis a gift from her father on his last day in the army.*

ELVIS & FRANK

"His kind of music is deplorable, a rancid-smelling aphrodisiac."

FRANK ON ELVIS, 1950s

Sinatra seemed to have changed his tune by 1960. Elvis' official TV comeback was to be on a Frank Sinatra special that the Colonel had arranged with ABC while Elvis was in Germany. Known as *Welcome Home, Elvis*, it was recorded on March 26 and was broadcast on May 12 between 9.30 and 10.30 pm. It was seen by a massive and unheard-of 41.5 percent of the country. Elvis may have been away for two years but this proved that he certainly hadn't been forgotten. While the Colonel hadn't allowed any live concerts while Elvis was in the army, a steady trickle of singles meant that his star could still be heard, although his fans were eager to see him in person. More than anything else, the show was evidence of Elvis' acceptance by a wider, older, and more conservative audience.

Elvis sang only two songs, "Stuck on You" and "Fame and Fortune"; Sinatra and Elvis dueted with Elvis singing "Witchcraft" and Sinatra tackling "Love Me Tender". The audience loved it. Nancy Sinatra appeared, as did the Rat Pack's Peter Lawford and Sammy Davis Jr.

Despite the shaky beginning, Elvis and Sinatra became friends and would later hang out together in Las Vegas. When Elvis died in 1977, Sinatra said: "There have been many accolades uttered about Elvis' talent and performances through the years, all of which I agree with wholeheartedly. I shall miss him dearly as a friend. He was a warm, considerate, and generous man."

GI BLUES
The movie

Elvis started shooting his fourth movie, *GI Blues*, in May and finished it in June. It was his first musical comedy and was one of nine movies produced for Paramount by Hal Wallis. Set in Germany, it was partly filmed while Elvis was serving in the army, although he took no part in these scenes. In fact, all of Elvis' scenes were shot on the set in Hollywood.

Mirroring Elvis' real-life army experience, his character, Tulsa Maclean, is a private in a tank regiment stationed in West Germany. Spurred on by his army buddies, he makes a bet that he can persuade beautiful cabaret dancer Lili (played by Frank Sinatra's real-life girlfriend, Juliet Prowse) to go out with him. She is known not to date soldiers but falls for Tulsa. However, when Lili realizes she has been the subject of a bet, she breaks up with him. All is resolved in the end fine in the end when Tulsa breaks off the bet after realizing that he truly loves her.

GI Blues was considered a decent romantic comedy and set the style for Elvis' future movies, nearly all of which were romantic comedies. As in Elvis' singing career, he was being steered toward a more wholesome image. The character of Tulsa was written for Elvis so that he would appeal to an older audience. The songs were gentler and there wasn't one controversial hip shake to be seen.

The movie was released in the United States on November 23, 1960, and peaked at No. 2 in the top grossing movies of that week. It ranked 14 in the United States annual ratings.

ELVIS AND THE THREE PRINCESSES
While on set, Elvis was visited by several sets of royalty, including the Danish royal family and their three princesses. Having met so many dignitaries, Elvis was not sure who he was meeting and, fearful of breaking protocol, asked "Is this another highness deal?"

The music

The album was a bestseller even though most modern critics rate it below *Elvis is Back* in terms of musical accomplishment. The soundtrack went to No. 1 in the United States. Recorded in Hollywood at RCA Studios and Radio Recorders, it was released in October 1960. In the movie, Elvis performs "Wooden Heart" during a date with Lili at a puppet show, singing in English and German while playing the accordion.

The most outstanding song is "Blue Suede Shoes", the Carl Perkins classic, which is played jokily in the movie. Tulsa is singing "Doin' the Best I Can" when a bored GI puts Elvis' "Blue Suede Shoes" on the jukebox. It had been a hit for him when released as a single in 1956. Along with the pop and rock songs, there were also some beautiful ballads in the movie, including "Pocket Full Of Rainbows", "Wooden Heart", and "Big Boots".

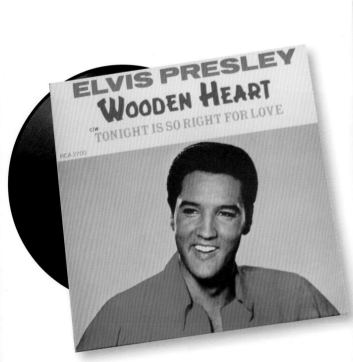

OPPOSITE AND RIGHT *Elvis in a scene from* GI Blues, *November 1960.*

IT'S NOW OR NEVER

Seen as a departure for Elvis in terms of musical style, "It's Now or Never" was his biggest selling international hit and a No. 1 on both sides of the Atlantic and in Australia. Elvis had always loved "O Sole Mio", as sung by Mario Lanza, one of his musical heroes, and his mother was said to have loved Enrico Caruso's version. While in the army, Elvis asked his music publisher Freddy Bienstock for new lyrics to be set to the Neapolitan opera-style "O Sole Mio", written in 1898. Aaron Schroeder and Wally Gold obliged and wrote the new lyrics for Elvis—his version became a classic in its own right. "It's Now or Never" was released on August 15, 1960, having been recorded on April 5 in Nashville.

Elvis' version is semi-operatic, his voice accompanied by mandolin and castanets. Once again, it shows a new type of Elvis sound—a far cry from his fifties rock 'n' roll classics. This was an Elvis who could sing well semi-operatically—something no one would have expected. In the United States, "It's Now or Never" reached a much wider audience than any of his previous releases and was played on radio stations that wouldn't have touched his pre-war music. Not everyone was happy, though; some critics thought Elvis had deserted rock 'n' roll.

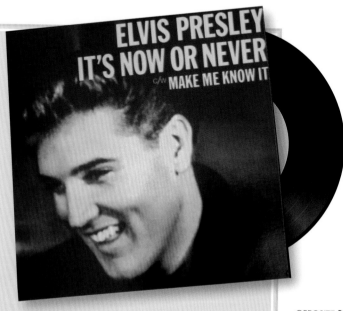

Facts

★ **B-Side:** "Mess of Blues"
★ **Recorded:** April 5, 1960
★ **Released:** August 15, 1960
★ **Label:** RCA Records
★ **Producer:** Steve Sholes

OPPOSITE *Portrait of Elvis taken around 1957.*

ARE YOU LONESOME TONIGHT?

Released in November 1960, "Are You Lonesome Tonight?" became a No. 1 hit on both sides of the Atlantic. The song was written in 1926 by Roy Turk and Lou Hardman and had been a hit for several artists, including Al Johnson. Elvis' version was based on one by the Blue Barron Orchestra in 1950. Part of the song was spoken: the words based on lines from Shakespeare's *As You Like It*—"All the world's a stage and all men and women merely players."

Elvis had recorded it in Nashville in April, along with "It's Now Or Never." Colonel Parker had encouraged Elvis to record it, as the Colonel's wife loved it. Wanting to capture the song's mellow feel, Elvis recorded it in the dark (apparently occasionally bumping into the microphone). He didn't like the recording and wanted it thrown out, but RCA producer Steve Sholes was happy with it and insisted it go ahead. It was a good call—"Are You Lonesome Tonight?" became one of the biggest selling singles of the year.

THE LAUGHING VERSION

In 1969, Elvis cracked up with laughter at a Vegas concert while singing the song. He was having fun with the lyrics and substituted the words "Do You Gaze At Your Doorstep/And Picture Me There?" with "Do You Gaze At Your Bald Head/And Wish You Had Hair?" Laughing at his own joke, he wasn't able to recover his composure for the duration of the song.

Facts

★ **B-Side:** "I Gotta Know"
★ **Recorded:** April 4, 1960
★ **Released:** November 1, 1960
★ **Label:** RCA
★ **Producer:** Steve Sholes

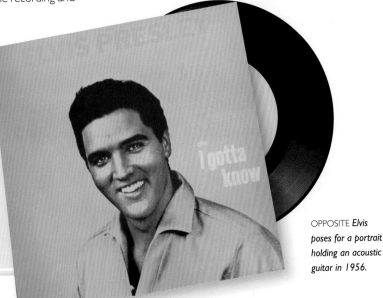

RCA 2699

OPPOSITE *Elvis poses for a portrait holding an acoustic guitar in 1956.*

89

FLAMING STAR

In September 1960, Elvis started shooting *Flaming Star* for Twentieth Century Fox. Directed by Don Siegel (who had directed *Invasion of the Body Snatchers* and went on to direct *Dirty Harry*), it was a serious drama with only two songs. The movie was based on a 1958 novel by Clair Huffaker, who also wrote for the TV series *Bonanza*. Frank Sinatra and Marlon Brando had originally been scheduled to play the brothers, but negotiations broke down between them and Fox and the part went to Elvis and another actor, Steve Forrest. Although *Flaming Star* was not a box office success, most critics felt that it showed Elvis to have raw acting talent.

Elvis plays Pacer Burton, who has a white father and a Native American Kiowa mother (played by the beautiful Mexican actress Dolores del Rio). He also has a half brother, Clint, who is white. Skirmishes between the whites and the Kiowa force Pacer and Clint to take sides. Pacer aligns himself with the Kiowa and Clint with the whites. Pacer's mother and father are killed and Pacer has to make another decision—to stay with the Kiowa or to save his half brother. He leaves the Kiowa and rescues Clint, but is fatally wounded and dies.

Flaming Star opened on December 22, 1960, but reached only No. 12 in the box office charts. Its lack of box-office success meant that Elvis was thereafter condemned to play in light-hearted romantic musicals, with the single exception of *Charro*, another Western in 1969. Speaking about *Flaming Star*, director Don Siegel said, in *Rolling Stone*, "They tried to get him [Elvis] to sing throughout the picture." He also said that he thought Elvis gave "… a beautiful performance."

Did You Know?

Andy Warhol's famous *Triple Elvis* screen print of Elvis, depicted as a cowboy pointing a gun, was taken from a still from the movie.

RIGHT *Elvis with Dolores Del Rio in a scene from the movie* Flaming Star, *1960.*

"... a beautiful performance."

DON SIEGEL, THE ROLLING STONE

the
USS ARIZONA
Memorial Benefit

"Our honored guest tonight is a fine American. He has had many starring roles. In one of these roles, his role as a soldier in the US Army, his performance was outstanding, and it's a great pleasure, to welcome him here, and to present to you ... Elvis Presley."

REAR ADMIRAL ROBERT L CAMPBELL,
INTRODUCING ELVIS AT THE USS ARIZONA
MEMORIAL BENEFIT

On March 25, 1961, Elvis was in Hawaii to give a benefit performance for the USS *Arizona* Memorial fund, at Bloch Arena, Pearl Harbor. The USS *Arizona* had been sunk in the Japanese attack on Pearl Harbor in 1941 with the loss of 1,177 lives. For many years, navy personnel had intended to raise money to build a fitting memorial to the servicemen who had died. The Colonel, perhaps charitably, or perhaps to gain good publicity for Elvis, suggested him for a charity concert to help raise the necessary funds. The one criterion was that all the proceeds from the concert went directly to the fund—this was met. Even the Colonel and Elvis bought tickets for themselves, as well as tickets for patients from the local army hospital.

It wasn't Elvis' first concert in Hawaii; he had given several before and had grown to love the islands. On his arrival, Elvis was mobbed by scores of teenage fans and presented with so many leis that at one point his face could barely be seen above them. He walked along the lines of fans, shaking hands and talking and signing autographs.

At the concert itself, Elvis wore a gold lamé jacket and performed 15 songs, including "Hound Dog" and "Heartbreak Hotel". He was at his peak, and the girls in the audience screamed as usual. The benefit raised $52,000 for the memorial fund.

The memorial was completed in May 1961 and, in 1965, Elvis and the Colonel visited it to lay wreaths. Elvis shooed away reporters, saying he wanted it to be a private moment.

This concert was Elvis' last live concert until 1968. After it, he stayed on in Hawaii to start filming *Blue Hawaii*.

OPPOSITE *Fans cluster around Elvis at Los Angeles airport before he flies off to Hawaii to star in* Blue Hawaii, *March 1961.*

1961–1967
ON LOCATION

Elvis, THE ACTOR

"I'd like to improve in an awful lot of ways … I try to do the best I can in movies."

ELVIS, 1962 INTERVIEW

Much has been written about Elvis in the movies. Could he really act? Did his roles let him down or was he really at his best in musical comedies? In total, he made 31 movies and many were made back-to-back, which meant that for half of his life as a famous entertainer, Elvis didn't perform live music—he just made movies. He set out to be the new James Dean but never made it anywhere close. The first movies he made were attempts to cast him as a serious actor, the new James Dean or Marlon Brando, whom he idolized. When they didn't do well at the box office, the Colonel seems to have decided that Elvis would never make it as a serious actor and Elvis seemed to accept this too.

From *Blue Hawaii* on, with the one exception of *Charro!*, Elvis was never again seen in a serious role or even a good movie. As the movies got worse, Elvis' appearance even changed: his hair got blacker and more and more sprayed, and his make-up made his skin look like plastic. He grew more and more disenchanted with the movie business. He was surrounded by friends and hangers on and became less approachable on set.

The choice of movie was decided by the studio (he had signed a contract with Paramount) and the Colonel, who was motivated by money and was completely uninterested in fostering any latent talent that Elvis might have had. Jerry Hopkins in his biography *Elvis* describes Elvis' film career in terms of "the Elvis Presley movie" and likens it to a "machine." Certainly, it must have seemed to Elvis in later years that he was stuck on a conveyor belt in a factory—albeit one that made movies.

We'll never really know what Elvis may have been capable of. What is clear is that, love it or loathe it, the "Elvis Presley movie" began in earnest with his next movie, *Blue Hawaii*.

LEFT *Dean Martin, Shirley MacLaine, and Elvis celebrated Martin's birthday on the set of* All in a Night's Work.

OPPOSITE *Elvis poses for a publicity still to promote the movie* Blue Hawaii, *in Los Angeles, California, 1961.*

BLUE HAWAII
The movie

Elvis was already in Hawaii for the USS *Arizona* Memorial benefit concert when shooting began on his seventh movie, *Blue Hawaii*. A light-hearted musical, it became Elvis' most commercially successful movie and the soundtrack was his best-selling movie album. It was directed by Norman Taurog, who had directed Elvis in *GI Blues*. Produced by Hal Wallis, it was released on November 22, 1961, and reached No. 8 in the United States box office polls for 1961.

Elvis plays Chad Gates, who has just been discharged from the army and is back in Hawaii with his friends and girlfriend, enjoying life as a surf dude. Chad's father and mother (the latter is played by a 35-year-old Angela Lansbury) want him to get a job at his family's business, the Great Southern Hawaiian Fruit Company, but instead Chad takes a job at his girlfriend's travel agency and hangs out with his beach buddies, considered undesirables by his mother. Eventually, Chad turns his life around by setting up his own travel agency and marries his girlfriend, thus winning his parents' approval.

The movie was filmed mainly on the islands of Oahu and Kauai, and the superb Hawaiian scenery alone makes it enjoyable viewing. The plot is absurd, but for some people it is one of Elvis's best movies.

Elvis was once again isolated by his fame, with thousands of fans hanging around the set and at his hotel, which meant that, instead of enjoying the islands he loved, he was forced to stay inside the hotel, which became a venue for nightly cast and crew parties. Hal Wallis decided to set a 10 o'clock curfew for the female cast members, who were turning up on set looking exhausted from partying the night before.

The music

"This should be the big one."

BILLBOARD'S REVIEW OF THE SOUNDTRACK ALBUM

A phenomenally successful soundtrack album, *Blue Hawaii* was recorded at Radio Recorders in Hollywood in March 1961—in just three sessions—and was released in October 1961. It spent a record 20 weeks at No. 1 in the United States Billboard pop chart and sold more than two million copies. In Britain, it was at No. 1 for 18 weeks.

The songs were mixed but some are critically acclaimed, including "Can't Help Falling In Love", considered a great Elvis love song and one that he later chose to close many of his 1970s concerts, and his reworking of "Blue Hawaii", originally a hit for Bing Crosby.

An authentic Hawaiian feel pervades the album. Some songs were traditional Hawaiian ballads, others were written specifically for the movie in a Hawaiian style. The evocative Hawaiian sound was achieved by using steel guitars and the ukulele, a traditional Hawaiian instrument, and Hawaiian musicians. The traditional Hawaiian song "Aloha Oe (Farewell to Thee)" was written by Liliuokalani, the last queen of Hawaii, which Elvis not only sang but also arranged skillfully.

A single with the A-side "Rock-A-Hula Baby" and the B-side "Can't Help Falling In Love" was released from the album. "Rock-A-Hula Baby", which was written for the movie, was a blend of rock song and Hawaiian folk song and became a popular dance tune.

The Album Tracks

★ "Blue Hawaii"
★ "Almost Always True"
★ "Aloha Oe"
★ "No More"
★ "Can't Help Falling In Love"
★ "Rock-A-Hula Baby"
★ "Moonlight Swim"
★ "Ku-u-i-po"
★ "Ito Eats"
★ "Slicin' Sand"
★ "Hawaiian Sunset"
★ "Beach Boy Blues"
★ "Island of Love"
★ "Hawaiian Wedding Song"

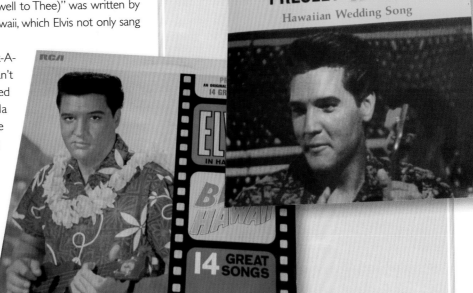

OPPOSITE *Still from the movie* Blue Hawaii, *1961.*

FOLLOW THAT DREAM

ALISHA CLAYPOOLE: "Has anyone ever told you you're very handsome?"

TOBY KWIMPER: "Only girls."

Elvis started shooting his ninth movie, *Follow That Dream*, in July 1961 on location in Florida and finished filming in August. The story was based on a novel by Richard Powell, *Pioneer, Go Home*. *Follow That Dream* was released in April 1962 and did well at the United States box office, reaching No. 5.

The tagline, which read "Elvis hits the road to laughter and hits a new high in romance," was pretty apt. Elvis plays Toby Kwimper, who, together with his southern hillbilly family (father and adopted siblings), travels to Florida and squats on an unopened part of a new highway, where the family decides to stay put. They manage to hang on to it despite many trials and tribulations and interference from the local authorities and a few mobsters. There is love interest for Elvis in the form of a beautiful social worker, played by Joanna Moore, who battles it out with Toby's childhood sweetheart, played by Ann Helm. His heart goes, naturally, to his childhood sweetheart in the end.

Kwimper was Elvis' first comedic character and, despite the reservations of many in the industry, he pulled it off, showing real ability for comedic timing.

Elvis, despite the heat (it often reached 100°F/37.8°C), enjoyed the filming. He cooled down in his air-conditioned white Cadillac, enjoyed his motorboat, and went water-skiing with his friends, known as the Memphis Mafia. He also romanced his co-star, Ann Helm.

BELOW *Elvis and three-year-old Pam Ogles on location at the movie* Follow That Dream *near Tampa, Florida.*

Did You Know?

A part of the highway where the movie was filmed was renamed *Follow That Dream.*

OPPOSITE *Elvis and Joanna Moore lying on a beach in* Follow That Dream, *1962.*

GIRLS! GIRLS! GIRLS! The movie

Elvis was back in Hawaii for the filming of *Girls! Girls! Girls!* in March 1962. Hal Wallis tried to recapture the success of *Blue Hawaii* and teamed up once again with its director, Norman Taurog.

Elvis plays Ross Carpenter, the skipper of a charter boat, who dreams of helping his father get back his sailing boat, which has been sold. Singing in a local nightclub is his only option and here he meets numerous girls, who all fight for his attention. One, the wealthy Laurel Dodge, played by Laurel Goodwin, secretly buys back the boat for him but, when Elvis discovers this he breaks up with her, only later to realize that he loves her.

One of Elvis' co-stars, Stella Stevens, who plays the hard nightclub singer Robin Ganter, who also falls for Elvis, hated doing the movie. She later reported that Elvis had been drinking heavily on set, which seems unlikely because Elvis didn't drink a lot. Stevens said that the whole experience was so bad she decided never to watch the movie.

Probably the most commercial movie Elvis had made to date, it really helped set the "Elvis" formula: beautiful scenery, Elvis singing his way through mostly mediocre songs, and lots of beautiful girls. It certainly wasn't his finest hour. But, as predicted by Paramount and the Colonel, it did very well at the box office, making $2.6 million and even being nominated for a Golden Globe award.

LEFT *Elvis and Stella Stevens on the set of* Girls! Girls! Girls!

The music

Recorded in March 1962 at Radio Recorders in Hollywood, the soundtrack for *Girls! Girls! Girls!* did well in the charts and is notable for one song in particular, "Return to Sender", which Elvis himself loved. Written by Otis Blackwell and Winfield Scott, it became a huge international hit for Elvis, going to No. 2 in the United States. The song is about a man who writes continuously to his girlfriend, who keeps returning his letters marked "Return to Sender". On January 8, 1993 a commemorative stamp was issued in the United States to celebrate Elvis' birthday. Many people posted incorrectly addressed letters with the Elvis stamp so that they would have them returned marked "Return to Sender".

The title track, "Girls! Girls! Girls!", was a Lieber and Stoller song that had previously been a hit for the Coasters. Elvis' version was well received by critics and is notable for Boots Randolph's baritone sax playing.

The soundtrack album also featured one the most bizarre songs that Elvis ever sang; "The Song of The Shrimp" is about a little shrimp saying goodbye to his shrimp parents and going to New Orleans for a better life, when actually he is heading for a shrimper's net. His fans loved it.

The album went to No. 3 in the Billboard pop chart.

The Album Tracks

★ "Girls! Girls! Girls!"
★ "I Don't Wanna Be Tied"
★ "Where Do You Come From?"
★ "A Boy Like Me, A Girl Like You"
★ "I Don't Want To"
★ "We'll Be Together"
★ "Earth Boy"
★ "Return to Sender"
★ "Because of Love"
★ "Thanks To The Rolling Sea"
★ "Song of the Shrimp"
★ "The Walls Have Ears"
★ "We're Comin' In"

ELVIS SINGS RETURN TO SENDER and WHERE DO YOU COME FROM?

RCA 2706

It Happened at THE WORLD'S FAIR

"Swinging higher than the space needle with the gals and the songs at the famous World's Fair."

TAGLINE TO MOVIE POSTER

Another month, another movie, again directed by Norman Taurog. This time Elvis was in Seattle with his entourage for filming in September 1962, and they stayed on the fourteenth floor of the New Washington Hotel. Before filming began, Elvis was fitted for a new wardrobe by leading Washington tailor Sy Devore. Devore said in an interview that Elvis' wardrobe for the movie cost $9, 300 and included ten suits and 55 ties.

Elvis plays Mike Edwards, a crop-duster pilot who, with his partner Danny Burke (played by Gary Lockwood), heads to the Seattle World's Fair to try to win back money to redeem their plane, which has been confiscated to pay off Danny's gambling debts. In Seattle, Mike ends up looking after a little girl, Sue-Lin (played by six-and-a-half-year-old Vicky Tui,) who has lost her father, and falling for nurse, Diane (played by Joan O'Brian), while Danny plays poker. One of the memorable moments in the movie is Kurt Russell's movie debut, when he gives Elvis a kick in the shins. Ironically, Russell went on to play Elvis in a TV movie directed by John Carpenter.

The movie was considered pretty mediocre. Released on April 3, 1963, it ranked No. 55 for the year on *Variety*'s list of top box office movies. The soundtrack album was also mediocre, and failed to reach the top ten in the United States.

While filming, Elvis' father and the mayor of Memphis visited the star on set and Elvis made his annual donation of $55,000 to Memphis charities.

ABOVE *Elvis and Joan O'Brien play nurse and patient in* It Happened at the World's Fair.

OPPOSITE *Elvis receives a manicure on Seattle's Monorail while filming* It Happened at the World's Fair.

PRISCILLA *in* GRACELAND

In June 1962, a 17-year old Priscilla visited Elvis in Las Vegas. She hadn't seen him since he left Germany two years earlier. In December, Elvis asked her to spend Christmas with him and his family in Graceland.

After this visit, it seems that Elvis made up his mind that he needed Priscilla more permanently in his life. First, however, he had to persuade her understandably reluctant parents. Somehow Elvis managed to get them to agree to let her live with his father and stepmother, emphasizing how much he respected their daughter and how well she would be chaperoned. She would live at Vernon and Dee's new house in Memphis.

In March, Priscilla and her stepfather flew to California, where Elvis was filming *Fun in Acapulco*. Captain Beaulieu had insisted that he meet Elvis face to face. They spent some time together, then Priscilla and her stepfather flew to Memphis to join Vernon and Dee. Priscilla was enrolled at the Immaculate Conception School in Memphis to finish her education. She graduated in May and had to talk Elvis out of attending the ceremony because of the chaos he would cause.

Under Elvis' direction, Priscilla dyed her hair jet black like his and took to wearing heavy eye make-up, which he liked—gradually he began to shape her into the woman he wanted her to be. Pretty soon, Priscilla had effectively moved into Graceland—after all, her parents were far away.

In August, as she was settling in, Elvis left her to start filming *Viva Las Vegas*.

LEFT *Priscilla Beaulieu helps Elvis' grandmother Minnie Mae Presley into her car. Priscilla got to know Elvis' extended family while in Germany.*

OPPOSITE *Elvis and his girlfriend and later wife Priscilla Beaulieu, 1968.*

FUN IN ACAPULCO

Released on November 27, 1963, *Fun in Acapulco* went to No. 5 in *Variety*'s weekly box office list and No. 33 in the annual list. The director was Richard Thorpe, who had directed *Jailhouse Rock*; the producer was Hal Wallis.

Filming started in January 1963. Elvis, however, stayed in Hollywood and didn't go to Mexico for the location shots, where a double was used.

Elvis plays Mike Windgren, a circus acrobat who has developed a fear of heights after causing serious injury to a fellow trapeze artist. He ends up in Mexico, where he finds work as a lifeguard during the day and as a singer at night. Here, as usual, two women vie for his attention, and he encounters hostility from a rival lifeguard.

Ursula Andress, the female star of the Bond movie *Dr No*, plays the woman who gets Elvis in the end, but only after he has conquered his fear of heights by diving off an ocean cliff. Elvis didn't perform this stunt but he did perform the trapeze stunt at the beginning of the movie. Hal Wallis agreed to let Elvis do it only if it was shot at the end of filming, in case he injured himself.

New York Times critic Howard Thompson seemed to like the movie well enough, saying: "Compared with the Beatles, Elvis Presley sounds like Caruso in *Fun in Acapulco* … And he certainly looks better."

A single released from the movie, "Bossa Nova Baby," sold well in the United States, going to No. 11 in the Billboard pop chart—the album went to No. 3. The album is now considered interesting because it allowed Elvis to explore his interest in Latin music.

> **"Compared with the Beatles, Elvis Presley sounds like Caruso in *Fun in Acapulco* … And he certainly looks better."**
>
> HOWARD THOMPSON, THE *NEW YORK TIMES*, 1963

RIGHT *Elvis and Ursula Andress in a still from the movie* Fun in Acapulco.

OPPOSITE *Elvis holds the hand of Ursula Andress in another still from the movie.*

VIVA LAS VEGAS

Filmed in August and September 1963 and released in May 1964, *Viva Las Vegas* was made for MGM. Directed by George Sidney, it became Elvis' biggest grossing movie, making $5.5 million at the box office. It was shot around Las Vegas—locations included the Flamingo Hotel and McCarran airport.

Everybody remembers *Viva Las Vegas* for the chemistry between Elvis and his co-star Ann-Margret. There was a problem at the beginning of filming because the Colonel thought Ann-Margret was getting too many close-ups—he complained to the director and the situation was resolved, but it is still, more than any other Elvis movie, a movie of two stars.

The story was formulaic. Elvis plays Lucky Jackson, a racing driver who comes to Vegas for a big race but with a broken engine. He takes a job as a waiter to earn money for his new engine, and meets and romances Rusty Martin, played by Ann-Margret, the hotel swimming pool manageress. He faces competition both on the race track and as a suitor for Rusty but gets the girl and wins the race. The movie was pacy and fun and the on-screen chemistry and fizz between the two stars made it very popular with the public.

THE SOUNDTRACK

The soundtrack was recorded at Radio Recorders in Hollywood in July 1963. "Viva Las Vegas", the title song, was released as a single but didn't do particularly well and, although Elvis performs brilliantly, a soundtrack album was never released. Of particular note are the title song, "C'mon Everybody", and "I Need Somebody to Lean On". Among the musicians for the recording session was the then unknown Glen Campbell.

> "**Coming on a balmy day, with no pretensions of art,** *Viva Las Vegas*, **the new Elvis Presley vehicle, is about as pleasant and as unimportant as a banana split.**"
>
> HOWARD THOMPSON,
> THE *NEW YORK TIMES*, MAY 1964

OPPOSITE *Elvis and Ann-Margret riding in a stock car in a scene from the movie* Viva Las Vegas.

ABOVE *Ann-Margret and Elvis dance for a promotional still for the movie* Viva Las Vegas, *1964.*

ELVIS &
ANN-MARGRET

There was a real romance between the two stars during filming, and the press and public loved it. Although it was built up in the papers (there was even a story that the stars had really married at their screen wedding and that Elvis had bought Ann-Margret a pink bed), it was an important relationship for both. You only have to look at their performance in "C'mon Everybody" to see how charismatic they were on screen, but in real life, too, they seemed good together. Elvis' friends, the so-called Memphis Mafia, liked Ann-Margret. Off screen she was good fun and light-hearted, one of the boys, and they all got on with her.

At the time, Elvis was still involved with Priscilla, who was back at Graceland. It's not clear whether or not he felt he had to make a choice, but the situation changed when Ann-Margret was reported as telling the press that she and Elvis were engaged. This was too much for Priscilla, who demanded to know what was going on, and Elvis broke off the relationship. However, he and Ann-Margret remained friends throughout his life and she described Elvis as a "soul mate." She became a big stage and screen star, winning many awards, including a Golden Globe for best actress in the movie *Tommy*. In 1967, she married actor Roger Smith.

Elvis sent her guitar-shaped bouquets before all of her concerts and she was the only one of Elvis' former girlfriends to attend his funeral.

RIGHT *Elvis and Ann-Margret rehearse a duet for the movie Viva Las Vegas.*

OPPOSITE *Ann-Margret and Elvis on the set of Viva Las Vegas, 1964.*

ROUSTABOUT

Produced by Hal Wallis, *Roustabout* was released in November 1964. It was No. 8 on *Variety*'s list of weekly top-grossing movies and made $3 million at the box office. Filming began in March 1964, with a formidable cast that included Barbara Stanwyck.

Elvis plays hard boy Charlie Rogers, a biking, coffee-bar singer with a chip on his shoulder. After a fight, he joins a carnival as a roustabout. The carnival is run by Maggie Morgan, played by Barabara Stanwyck. Elvis' singing brings in new customers and Elvis soon falls for Cathy, the co-manager's daughter, played by Joan Freeman. After getting into trouble, he leaves for a rival carnival. However, he returns to help the now failing circus and win his girl.

While on the shoot, Elvis was crushed to learn that a newspaper article had appeared saying that the Elvis money-making machine financed more serious movies made by Paramount. Although he must already have known it, this just confirmed that he wasn't ever going to be taken seriously as a movie star.

Terri Garr and Raquel Welch both make appearances in this movie. In an interview with the *Ladies Home Journal* (2007), Raquel Welch said of Elvis that "He was more packaged. His clothes were not the same, his hair was obviously dyed now, and it was sprayed into place … It was a whitewashed, cleaned-up Elvis …"

ROUSTABOUT, THE ALBUM

The soundtrack album went to No. 1 in the United States for one week, though it is generally dismissed by the critics; its best song was the Lieber and Stoller number "Little Egypt", though even this was never released as a single. It was Elvis' last No. 1 album for eight years.

RIGHT *Barbara Stanwyck and Elvis during a break in filming* Roustabout, *April 1964.*

Did You Know?

Elvis insisted on doing his own stunts for the movie and was injured in a fight scene. The producer quickly wrote in a crash scene to explain Elvis' bandage above his eye.

GIRL HAPPY

Howard Thompson just about sums it up. *Girl Happy* began shooting in June 1964, and was released on April 7, 1965. It reached No. 25 on *Variety's* list of box-office hits, and its soundtrack album reached No. 8 on the Billboard pop chart. It wasn't the worst Elvis movie, but most critics felt that it lacked spark.

Elvis plays Rusty Wells, a nightclub singer with a band, who is asked by his boss, Big Frank, to watch over his daughter, Valerie (played by Shelley Fabares), on her spring break in Fort Lauderdale, Florida. Rusty's attempts to find romance are continuously interrupted by having to watch out for Valerie. Of course, eventually, they fall for each other.

Elvis had a good rapport with his co-star, Shelley, who was later to appear in two other Presley movies. Although they never dated, they formed a close relationship.

ELVIS AND LARRY

By the time he was filming *Girl Happy*, Elvis was completely disillusioned with the movie business. He now firmly believed that he would never be given the chance to develop as a serious actor. Feeling low, he began to examine a growing interest in spiritual ideas. He had a new hairdresser, Larry Geller, who happened to be interested in religion, and Geller soon became an important part of Elvis' entourage. Although officially a member of the Pentecostal Church since childhood, and a Bible reader (he knew whole passages off by heart), Elvis was encouraged by Geller to read a range of mystical books, such as *The Prophet*, by Kahlil Gibran, and Joseph Benner's *The Impersonal Life*. Geller's influence lasted until Elvis' death.

RIGHT *Elvis Presley and Mary Ann Mobley star in* Girl Happy.

TICKLE ME

"The silliest, feeblest, and dullest vehicle for the Memphis Wonder in a long time."

HOWARD THOMPSON, THE *NEW YORK TIMES* 1965

Tickle Me was the only movie Elvis made for an ailing Allied Artists, and it actually saved them from bankruptcy. Directed by the old Elvis hand, Norman Taurog, it was released in June 1965. It stands out as the only Elvis movie for which no new songs were written—all the songs had been recorded between 1960 and 1963. Other cost-cutting schemes were put into place to prevent the studio from going under: the movie was shot entirely in the back lot of the studio and the Colonel agreed to cut Elvis' fee.

Shooting began in October 1964. Elvis plays Lonnie Beale, a singing rodeo cowboy, who also works at a beauty ranch as a handyman. Several women vie for his attention but he falls for Pam Merrit, played by Jocelyn Lane. Pam is in town to find a cache of gold hidden by her grandfather. Lonnie helps Pam look for it, and, despite adversity and many setbacks, they recover the gold and marry at the end of the movie.

Howard Thompson of the *New York Times* called it "the silliest, feeblest, and dullest vehicle for the Memphis Wonder in a long time." Fans seemed to agree, since it didn't do well at the box office and it didn't appear in *Variety*'s list of top-grossing movies.

RIGHT *Elvis Presley with co-star Jocelyn Lane in the 1964 movie* Tickle Me.

The Album Tracks

★ "Lonely, Lonely Highway"

★ "It Feels So Right"

★ "(Such An) Easy Question"

★ "I'm Yours"

★ "I Feel That I've Known You Forever"

★ "Slowly But Surely"

★ "Night Rider"

★ "Put The Blame On Me"

★ "Dirty, Dirty Feeling"

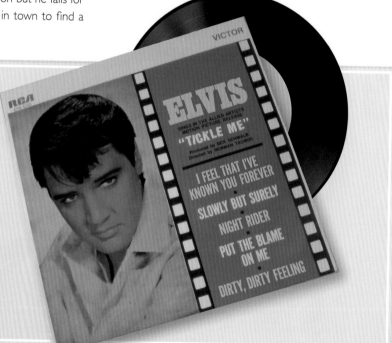

HARUM SCARUM

"...the animation of a man under deep sedation, but then he had read the script..."

VINCENT CANBY, THE NEW YORK TIMES, 1965

Made in just over two weeks by MGM in March 1965, and thought of as his most bizarre, if not his worst movie, *Harum Scarum* (*Harem Holiday* in Britain) still managed to make $2 million at the box office and the soundtrack went to No. 8 in the Billboard charts.

The improbable storyline concerns a singing star and movie idol, Johnny Tyrone, who is kidnapped in the Middle East and is forced by his abductors to try to kill the king of Lunarkand. He finds he can't do it (and doesn't want to it) and also falls in love with a slave, who turn out to be the king's daughter, Princess Shalimar, played by Mary Ann Mobley. It ends with Tyrone escaping his kidnappers and launching a new Las Vegas act with a troupe of harem beauties. It was released in November 1965, and even the Colonel found it hard to take. He suggested that the plot might be helped along by the introduction of a talking camel—which, fortunately, didn't happen.

For the movie, Elvis dressed like Valentino, a star he admired, and looked suitably debonair. However, nothing could hide the ludicrousness of the plot and the banality of the songs. To save money, the sets and the costumes were reused from earlier movies; the former had been used in MGM's *King of Kings* and the latter in *Kismet*.

ABOVE *Mary Ann Mobley at a Hollywood event in 1965.*

OPPOSITE *Elvis wearing a traditional Arabian headress to publicize the release of* Harum Scarum, *February 1965.*

PARADISE, HAWAIIAN STYLE

ABOVE *Elvis in Hawaii with actress Marianna Hill, one of his co-stars in* Paradise, Hawaiian Style, *January 1965.*

OPPOSITE *Elvis and James Shigeta in a still from the movie* Paradise, Hawaiian Style.

Another Hal Wallis production, *Paradise, Hawaiian Style*, was Elvis' third movie to be set and filmed on Hawaii and was an attempt to repeat the success of *Blue Hawaii*. Shooting commenced in August 1965. Elvis was ill on the first day of recording and so his vocals were dubbed in later. *Movie News*, who saw him arrive in Hawaii, noted that he was "without his usual smiling face …" He was also overweight at the beginning of shooting, but lost weight as the movie progressed.

Elvis plays Greg "Rick" Richards, a pilot who sets up his own charter helicopter business with his partner Danny (played by James Shigeta) and charms women all over the Hawaiian islands. At the office, beautiful Judy Hudson (played by Suzanna Leigh) is the girl Friday. To avoid romantic complications, Danny tells Rick she is married. After a mix-up, Rick loses his pilot's permit, but when he fears his partner is in trouble, he defies the ban against him and flies off to find and save Danny. Rick falls in love with Judy and discovers that she isn't really married.

Several scenes were filmed in the Polynesian Cultural Center, where Elvis and other cast and crew members learned about Hawaiian traditions and culture. At the end of filming, the centre hosted a party in which they put on a dance recital; Elvis was seen leaving the party covered in leis and crying, greatly moved by the event.

Released in June 1966, *Paradise, Hawaiian Style* received poor reviews and reached only No. 40 in *Variety*'s list of annual box-office successes. The soundtrack did moderately well and went to No. 15.

Elvis &
THE FAB FOUR

"Before Elvis, there was nothing."

JOHN LENNON

In April 1964, when Elvis was making *Roustabout*, the Beatles were having a hit single on both sides of the Atlantic with "Can't Buy Me Love". Elvis admired but slightly feared the British band, but the Beatles were in awe of the King. On a visit to Los Angeles in 1965, when Beatlemania was at its peak, they were eager to meet him. By all accounts, the impetus for the meeting came from theirs and not Elvis' side. Elvis had just finished shooting *Paradise, Hawaiian Style* and was at his Los Angeles home.

The meeting didn't go too well initially; the Beatles were ushered in but Elvis continued to watch television for the first 30 minutes or so, until he eventually said that if they didn't want to talk he was going to bed. The ice broken, they chatted and joked and eventually jammed together, with Elvis playing the bass, which he had been learning for a while. They also played roulette and pool. John Lennon asked Elvis if he would visit them at their rented LA house, but Elvis didn't take them up on the offer and they never met again, although George Harrison did go to some of Elvis' later concerts. The meeting lasted around four hours.

Lennon later recalled that he and Elvis were both big fans of Peter Sellers. When he left the room, his final words to Elvis were (in a Peter Sellers voice), "Tanks for ze music, Elvis—and long live ze king."

It is also said that John and Elvis exchanged phone numbers and that they may have spoken on the phone after the meeting. Since no one had brought a camera, there are no pictures from the event.

LEFT *The Beatles at a London Airport as they leave for a tour of the United States, 1964.*

OPPOSITE *Elvis poses for a portrait, 1962.*

SPINOUT

Filming for this MGM production, directed by Norman Taurog, began in February 1966. There had been trouble finding a title for the movie: *Clambake* (suggested by the Colonel), *Jim Dandy,* and *After Midnight* were all mooted.

In a reprise of *Viva Las Vegas*, Elvis plays a racing driver and singer, Mike McCoy, who has to fight off the attentions of three women. One of these is played by Shelley Fabares, who had co-starred with him in *Girl Happy*. Unusually for an Elvis movie, he doesn't get married at the end. Instead, he manages to marry all three women off to other men, and is free to pursue a new romance.

Spinout was released in October 1966 and went to No. 57 in the annual box-office charts. The soundtrack album went to No. 18.

MGM publicity mimicked part of the storyline to promote the movie. In the movie, one of the women pursuing Elvis, Diana St Clair (played by Diane McBain), is writing a book entitled *The Perfect American Male*. In real life, cinemas held essay-writing contests on *The Perfect American Male*, with the winners receiving free Elvis albums.

Did You Know?

It was on this movie that Elvis began a long musical collaboration with musician James Burton, who played on the *Spinout* soundtrack album. Burton, a self-taught guitarist, was later to join Elvis' band, playing from 1969 to 1977. He is said never to have missed a show.

RIGHT *Portrait of actress Diane McBain, taken in 1965.*

DOUBLE TROUBLE

MGM's *Double Trouble* was Elvis' twenty-fourth movie and was, once again, directed by Norman Taurog. Filming took place from June to September 1966.

Elvis stars as singer Guy Lambert, who is performing in London when a wealthy but innocent heiress, Jill Conway (played by Annette Day), falls for him. Her father sends her to Antwerp, Belgium, to prevent a relationship, but his plans go awry when Guy starts a singing tour in the same city. There they become tangled up with jewel thieves and all sorts of capers. Eventually, everything is rectified and they marry. Despite the European setting, Elvis and Day never left California—body doubles were used on location in Belgium. At the end of shooting, Elvis gave his co-star Annette Day a white Mustang convertible, but since she couldn't drive she gave it to her brother. This was the only film that Day ever made.

The movie was meant to cash in on the Swingin' London scene, the Beatles' *Hard Day's Night*, and the Bond movies. However, it missed the target spectacularly. Once again, Elvis was dismayed by the banality of the script and the songs. When he was forced to sing "Old Macdonald" he walked out before it was finished, so the movie contains a very short, unfinished version.

The movie was released in April 1967. It reached No. 58 on *Variety*'s list.

Elvis later said about the film: "I wasn't exactly a James Bond in this movie. But then, no one ever asked Sean Connery to sing a song while dodging bullets."

ABOVE *Elvis with Annette Day in* **Double Trouble.**

EASY COME, EASY GO

Considered one of the lowest points of his movie career, this was the last of Elvis' movies to be produced by Hal Wallis. Shooting began in October 1966 and locations included the Paramount lot and the Long Beach Naval Station. The ship shown at the beginning of the movie is the USS *Gallant*, a minesweeper.

Elvis plays a navy diver, Ted Jackson. He is about to leave the navy, but on one of his final dives he discovers a wreck and a treasure chest. Ted tries to finds out what is in the chest and is led to a woman called Jo Symington, played by Dodie Marshall, who is a descendant of the ship's captain. She believes the chest will contain gold coins and asks Jackson to help her retrieve it so she can donate it to a local community arts initiative. When the chest is finally opened, it contains copper, but Ted donates it anyway and wins Jo's heart.

The experience on this movie was not good for Elvis. He didn't work well with the director, John Rich, who had also directed *Roustabout*, and who didn't appreciate Elvis' entourage, and he hated the songs. Elvis turned up late for the first day of recording the soundtrack. The soundtrack was released as an extended play single and sold only 30,000 copies.

Easy Come, Easy Go was released in March 1967 and reached No. 50 in the box office charts in the United States. However, almost inexplicably, the reviews were quite good.

LEFT *Elvis in full SCUBA gear for the movie* Easy Come, Easy Go, *1967.*

1967–1968
FAMILY LIFE
& MORE MOVIES

ELVIS PROPOSES

For Priscilla, life at Graceland was not quite what she had expected—Elvis was regularly away filming—and then there were constant whisperings about the other women in his life. She was often alone with his staff and paternal grandmother (known as Grandma Dodger). Life without Elvis was quite suffocating; Vernon drove her around until she could drive and gave her pocket money. But she found him a little distant and hard to get to know. She lived for Elvis' phone calls and breaks from filming. However, even when Elvis was home, he was continuously surrounded by his entourage, which Priscilla found infuriating. He would become one of the boys and transform into an Elvis she didn't really know, although he assured her in their private moments that she knew the "real" person. A certain amount of animosity developed between Priscilla and the Memphis Mafia. By all accounts, not all of Elvis' entourage were happy about her growing influence.

Then, in December 1966, Priscilla's patience was rewarded; Elvis got down on one knee and proposed to her. He gave her a 3.33-carat diamond ring, encircled by detachable diamonds.

There has been much debate as to whether Elvis really wanted to get married (he had always spoken ambivalently on the subject) or whether the Colonel had prompted him to do so because he feared Elvis' image was suffering from having, to all intents and purposes, a live-in lover. There was also pressure from Priscilla's family. And, while Elvis loved her, he was continuing to have numerous other relationships.

BELOW *Priscilla and Elvis on holiday in Hawaii.*

RIGHT *Priscilla with her poodle in 1960.*

LIFE at the RANCH

In February 1967, Elvis bought a 167-acre (67.6-ha) farm in Mississippi. Originally called Twinkletown Farm, he renamed it Circle-G, in homage to his beloved Graceland. Elvis had seen the ranch while out driving and had fallen in love with the place. It was about 10 miles (16 km) away from Graceland, and in Mississippi, the state of his birth. He already had horses at Graceland but wanted more room for this growing passion. He named his barn the House of the Rising Sun after a beloved palomino horse, Rising Sun. When Rising Sun died, he was buried facing the rising sun. Elvis also bought a horse called Domino for Priscilla, who turned out to be a natural horsewoman.

With typical generosity, Elvis bought horses for his friends and their wives and girlfriends; he was said to have spent $1 million on horses in one week. He also bought trailers for the ranch, almost turning the property into a commune.

Elvis loved life at Circle-G; it became a place of relaxation for him, his entourage, and their wives. It was a great antidote to the madness of Hollywood and the lack of privacy at Graceland. For Priscilla, however, it was really just another place that the whole gang could get together—once again, she found that she couldn't be alone with Elvis. The only exception to this was their honeymoon.

Elvis sold the ranch after just two years. He had become bored with it and the maintenance costs were escalating. In 2005, despite protests from the public, it was sold to developers.

RIGHT *Elvis and Priscilla boarding a chartered jet airplane on their honeymoon—one of the few times they were alone together.*

CLAMBAKE

Released in November 1967, *Clambake* was another very poor movie that Elvis really complained about. Shooting started in March, but it was held up for two weeks when the star slipped and banged his head in his Los Angeles home, suffering a concussion. Elvis was still overweight; United Artists told him he had to lose it, so Elvis added diet pills to the amphetamines that he had started to take in Germany. For Elvis, one of the few good things about the movie was that his co-star was Shelley Fabares, who had appeared in *Girl Happy* and *Spinout*, and with whom he had a good working relationship.

In *Clambake*, Elvis played Scott Heyward, the son of an oil magnate, who trades places with a waterskiing instructor, Tom Wilson (played by Will Hutchins), to see if he can be a success without money and influence. Tom, on the other hand, wants to see what it is like to be rich. Shelley Fabares plays the girl that Scott falls for, a girl who is looking for a rich husband.

The movie was set in Florida but was filmed in California. Numerous errors were made concerning the location, not least of all the fact that Californian mountains are visible in several scenes. There are no mountains in Florida—something the critics didn't fail to point out.

The movie peaked at No. 15 in the weekly *Variety* list and the soundtrack album made it to No. 40. Elvis was once again paid his usual $1 million fee, but for the last time.

> ## "Elvis Presley hit a real Christmas clinker yesterday with *Clambake*, a silly, tired little frolic that could have used a few clams."
>
> HOWARD THOMPSON, THE *NEW YORK TIMES*, DECEMBER 1967

LEFT *Elvis singing with guitar in the movie* Clambake.

HOW GREAT THOU ART

In February 1967, when Elvis was in some despair over his career, an album he had made in 1966, and which he had been excited about, was released to great critical acclaim. He had recorded it at the RCA studio in Nashville at a time when all his recordings were for movie soundtrack albums. *How Great Thou Art* was Elvis' second gospel album, but it was his first to go to platinum. It won a Grammy award for Best Sacred Performance, the first of Elvis' three Grammy wins. Produced by Felton Jarvis, it marked the beginning of a new and highly successful musical collaboration for Elvis. In 1970, Jarvis left RCA to work exclusively for Elvis, producing his records for the rest of the star's life.

Elvis insisted on having certain musicians and singers on the album and took charge of the recording in a way that he hadn't done for several years. The result, most critics agree, shows how much Elvis truly cared about his music, particularly gospel.

FELTON JARVIS

Jarvis had seen Elvis perform in the fifties and had been fascinated by him. He even attempted to imitate him and, in 1959, produced an Elvis tribute which was called "Don't Knock Elvis". Jarvis and Elvis not only developed a close musical collaboration but also a close friendship.

The Album Tracks

★ "How Great Thou Art"
★ "In the Garden"
★ "Somebody Bigger Than You and I"
★ "Farther Along"
★ "Stand By Me"
★ "Without Him"
★ "So High"
★ "Where Could I Go But To The Lord"
★ "By And By"
★ "If The Lord Wasn't By My Side"
★ "Run On"
★ "Where No One Stands Alone"
★ "Crying In The Chapel"

RIGHT *Elvis in a publicity photo, taken in Los Angeles, around 1966.*

the WEDDING

Eight years after they had first met, Elvis and Priscilla were married on May 1, 1967, in a private ceremony at the Aladdin Hotel in Las Vegas, with just close family and friends present. The wedding came as a surprise to the press and, after the ceremony, there was a press conference. The *Las Vegas Sun* reported on May 2 that after the ceremony, there was an elaborate banquet held just below the hotel's casino. An estimated 100 guests dined on ham, eggs, Southern fried chicken, oysters Rockefeller, roast suckling pig, poached and candied salmon, lobster, eggs Minette, and champagne.

Elvis wore a black silk tuxedo and Priscilla a white chiffon gown that she had designed herself. The wedding cake had six tiers and was 5 feet (1.5m) high. Priscilla's sister Michelle was her bridesmaid and two of the Memphis Mafia, Jo Esposito and Marty Lacker, acted as best men. A second wedding reception was held at Graceland on May 29 for those who had been unable to get to Las Vegas. However, many of the Memphis Mafia hadn't been invited to the wedding, including Elvis' old school friend Red West. Elvis' relationship with West and many of the Memphis Mafia was never the same again after this.

The honeymoon was split between a few days in Palm Springs and couple of weeks on Elvis' beloved ranch—it was one of the first times that Priscilla and Elvis were on their own for any length of time. After the honeymoon, Elvis bought a new home in California for himself and his new wife. It was located in an exclusive development on a mountainside in Beverly Hills and offered some privacy for the couple.

OPPOSITE AND RIGHT *Elvis and Priscilla on their wedding day, May 1, 1967.*

PRISCILLA IS PREGNANT

Priscilla realized she was pregnant just before the group left Memphis in Elvis' souped-up tour bus to make their way to California for the production of his next movie, *Speedway*. The journey became a fun trip for Elvis, Priscilla, and their friends. Priscilla, however, felt ambivalent about the pregnancy; she had hoped that for some time at least she and Elvis could be together without too many interruptions or obligations, and was worried that Elvis would feel similarly ambivalent. However, he was unequivocally delighted and immediately told Vernon that he would soon be a grandfather.

In her book *Elvis and Me*, Priscilla says that she was so worried about letting herself go—something Elvis complained that many women did—that she actually managed to lose weight during her pregnancy.

Elvis announced his wife's pregnancy on July 12, during the filming of *Speedway*. He told reporters, "This is the greatest thing that has ever happened to me." At the time he was said to be having an affair with his co-star Nancy Sinatra, which Priscilla heard about. It can't have helped her unease when Elvis gave Nancy a car with "Speedway" painted on one side and "Starring Elvis and Nancy" on the other, or when Nancy phoned Priscilla to ask if she could give her a baby shower.

Seven months into the pregnancy, and completely out of the blue, Elvis stunned Priscilla by asking for a trial separation, saying that he needed some space. She didn't know what to make of it, but having mentioned it once, he never brought up the subject again.

RIGHT *Elvis with Nancy Sinatra and the cast of* Speedway *just after Priscilla announced her pregnancy, June 1967.*

"This is the greatest thing that has

ever happened to me."

ELVIS TO REPORTERS, JULY 1967

SPEEDWAY

Shot in July and August 1967, *Speedway* was directed by Norman Taurog and produced by MGM.

Elvis plays an overly generous stock-car racing champion, Steve Grayson, who just can't help giving away his winnings to worthy causes. In addition, he has a bumbling manager who gambles. He discovers he owes the government back taxes and is forced to budget in order to pay them. Beautiful IRS agent, Susan Jacks, played by Nancy Sinatra, is sent to spy on him. Steve tries to woo her, but she is intent only on doing her job and recovering the taxes. However, when she discovers that one of Steve's worthy causes is to help an ex-stock car racer and his five children, she helps him keep to a budget, and he wins her heart.

The movie, released on June 12, 1968, reached No. 40 on *Variety*'s top-grossing movies for the year, and the soundtrack album reached No. 80 in the Billboard charts.

ELVIS AND NANCY

The two had met on Elvis' return from Germany in March 1960 at the McGuire Airforce Base, where Nancy Sinatra greeted Elvis officially on his return; she had presented him with two shirts as a present from her father. They then both appeared on the *Frank Sinatra Special* in May. On the *Speedway* soundtrack, Nancy sang a duet with Elvis, which was released on the album. This was the first time that an Elvis album had ever featured a guest singer. Although Ann-Margret had dueted with Elvis in *Viva Las Vegas*, contractual restrictions meant that the duets were released only after Elvis' death.

BELOW *Elvis and Nancy Sinatra pose for a still while filming Speedway.*

LEFT *Elvis poses for a still while filming the movie* Speedway, *1967.*

STAY AWAY JOE

A comedy western with a handful of songs, *Stay Away Joe* sees Elvis playing a Native American for the second time. Joe Lightcloud is a rodeo rider who returns home to his Navajo reservation after persuading a local congressman to let him have a herd of cattle to prove that the Navajo were capable of raising cattle. However, when the prize bull is barbecued and Joe sells some of the cattle to buy items for his stepmother's home, the plans go awry. In the end, though, Joe saves the day.

Elvis hoped that the part, though comedic, would help him grow as an actor, and the supporting cast, which included veterans Burgess Meredith and Joan Blondell, was of the highest quality. However, the movie missed its target and was lambasted by the critics. In addition, the portrayal of the Navajo as irresponsible and feckless led to criticisms of racial stereotyping.

Stay Away Joe was filmed from October to November 1967 in Arizona, and Elvis, Priscilla, and the members of a now dwindling entourage stayed on location. Elvis was slim and tanned for the movie and, despite hating one of the songs ("Dominick," sung to a bull), he seemed to enjoy the experience. Elvis asked that the offending song would not be released during his lifetime.

The movie was released by MGM on March 8, 1968, and went to No. 65 on *Variety*'s list of annual best-selling movies. There were only five songs in the movie and no accompanying soundtrack album was released. Even the Colonel sensed that something had to change and, behind the scenes, he was arranging a Christmas television special for Elvis.

ABOVE *Elvis with Quentin Dean in Stay Away Joe, 1968.*

OPPOSITE *Elvis poses in a publicity still for Stay Away Joe.*

LIVE A LITTLE, LOVE A LITTLE

The ninth and last movie Elvis made with director Norman Taurog, *Live A Little, Love A Little*, was an attempt at a screwball comedy that didn't really succeed. It was a more adult movie than Elvis' previous ones, with references to drugs and an exhibition of bad language by Elvis' character, making it something of a departure for him. He seemed, finally, and belatedly, to be taking a chance with his screen persona.

The movie was filmed from March to May 1968. Elvis plays Greg Nolan, a newspaper photographer who enjoys his carefree life until he meets a strange woman called Bernice (played by Michele Carey), who seems to have a long list of different names. She causes chaos in his life and manages to lose his job—but even so he falls for her. The script allows for plenty of opportunity for comedic mix-ups and farce.

During filming, Elvis learned of the assassination of Martin Luther King Jr in Memphis on April 4. Elvis knew King's speeches by heart and was greatly upset by the news.

Live A Little, Love A Little was released on October 28, 1968, but it didn't do well at the box office.

"A LITTLE LESS CONVERSATION"

No soundtrack album was released, but the best song on the movie soundtrack, "A Little Less Conversation", was released as a single. However, at the time, it didn't even reach the Top 40. A remixed version was released in 2002—it became a huge hit.

OPPOSITE *Elvis with Celeste Yarnell in* Live a Little, Love a Little, *1968.*

RIGHT *Marchers in Memphis carry signs to mourn Martin Luther King Jr after his assassination. Elvis was greatly affected by the news.*

the LITTLE PRINCESS

On February 1, 1968, Lisa Marie Presley was born at the Baptist Memorial Hospital in Memphis, exactly nine months to the day after her parents' wedding. She weighed in at 6 pounds and 15 ounces (1.4kg). With security guards in place at the hospital to keep the fans away, the delivery lasted nine hours, while Elvis, predictably, paced the hospital floor. About a dozen members of his entourage were also at the hospital—after the birth, an ecstatic Elvis handed around cigars. Priscilla said that if it had been a boy they would have named him John Barron.

Elvis and Priscilla left the hospital after four days. Priscilla can be seen in photos with her hair in a large bouffant, make-up carefully applied. Elvis was beaming as the press took photos and fans waved. Thousands of cards and baby gifts were sent to Graceland. For the first few days, Elvis was hardly able to put Lisa Marie down. He was to become a doting and generous father.

After a month, Elvis and Priscilla left Graceland for California. Elvis started shooting his next movie *Live A Little, Love A Little,* while Priscilla settled into a new home in Hillcrest, Beverly Hills. From this point onward Elvis and Priscilla would move between Graceland and Hillcrest. With fewer of the Memphis Mafia around, their lives seemed more settled than usual. Priscilla was able to create something of a more normal domestic life.

Elvis' pet names for Lisa were "Buttonhead' and "Yisa." Family photos and home movies show the Presleys as a happy smiling couple, with their adored daughter. This was part of the truth and, in the months following Lisa's birth, both Elvis and Priscilla were outwardly happier and more relaxed than ever before.

For the next few years, their lives were, however, far from normal. Elvis lived a largely nocturnal lifestyle, waking at about 4 o'clock in the afternoon, and staying up for most of the night until around 5 o'clock in the morning—not an easy lifestyle for the mother of a small child. And, during this period, although the family had more privacy than before, there were always fans at the gates of Graceland; Elvis would take time every day to chat with them and sign autographs.

Although Elvis was loving and kind, he had a bad temper, which he himself admitted. Priscilla has also written about his controlling streak: she couldn't even look at other men if Elvis wasn't in the mood. A doting father, Elvis' generosity toward his infant daughter was excessive. On one birthday, he hired Libertyland, an amusement park, for Lisa and her friends, and on another he bought her a pony, which she was allowed to ride through the doors at Graceland.

An almost nightly habit was what became known as the "Midnight Movies." Elvis would hire a cinema for family and friends to enjoy several movies, starting from midnight. Sometimes up to 50 friends would be invited along.

Everything, it seems, was on a big scale.

OPPOSITE *Elvis and Priscilla with their daughter, Lisa Marie in Memphis on February 5, 1968.*

Family life

Family shots of the Presleys just after the birth of their daughter Lisa Marie at the Baptist Hospital in Memphis, Tennessee (see below) on February 5, 1968, show they were perhaps as happy and as relaxed as they had ever been.

Elvis doted on his daughter (see right) and Priscilla had a focus for her life while Elvis was away shooting movies.

Overview—EARLY 1968

In early 1968, the Beatles had had a string of hits both sides of the Atlantic, with their "Lady Madonna" going to No. 1 in the United States and Britain. Elvis was keenly aware that it was they who were leading the swinging sixties music scene. His last No. 1 hit had been in 1962.

He was now married with a daughter, and had developed an interest in spiritual matters, but no amount of distraction could prevent him from realizing that his career was in a downward spiral. On March 8, his latest movie, *Stay Away Joe*, was released to terrible reviews and produced no accompanying soundtrack album. Elvis realized that he had to get back to performing live—all he had ever wanted to do was to entertain people, and his movies, as he must have been aware, were not achieving this.

The Colonel, too, realized that Elvis' career was in danger of collapsing, and that something needed to be done; finally it was accepted that Elvis' extraordinary charisma didn't come across on celluloid. The Colonel's response to the situation was an anodyne Christmas special with NBC. Elvis agreed, but didn't want a mellow affair with "Christmas" songs—in fact, it transpired after much discussion that the only person who wanted a traditional Christmas show was Colonel Parker. Elvis wanted rock 'n' roll. Eventually, the Colonel relented—there would just one "Christmassy" number on the show.

The agreement was made on January 12, 1968, with NBC. Elvis would be paid $250,000 for the special, his first TV appearance in eight years.

BELOW *Elvis performing live for an NBC television special in 1968.*

1968–1969
THE COMEBACK KID

the '68 COMEBACK SPECIAL

"If ever there was a music that bleeds, this was it."

MARCUS GRIEL, MUSIC EDITOR AND JOURNALIST

To say that the 1968 special was a milestone in Elvis' career is almost to underestimate its importance, both for Elvis' career and the development of the TV music special. It could be argued that we might not remember Elvis today as the "King" if he hadn't made this spectacular piece of television, which also introduced the idea of the informal jamming session to a TV audience.

The special was officially called *Elvis*, although it became known as the "'68 Comeback Special." Rehearsals began in June and the show was recorded in July. Elvis was slim and fit for the show; at 33, he looked more handsome than ever, and his voice was in great shape.

The show was to have an intimate atmosphere, with a small audience to which Elvis spoke directly, telling stories and explaining songs. For the jamming sessions that ran through the special, Elvis, resplendent in a black leather suit, was presented on a small square surrounded on four sides by his audience. He sat among them and sang directly to them. He seemed to be in his element.

A semi-autobiographical theme ran through the show, epitomized by the song "Guitar Man", which Elvis had first recorded in 1967. In "Guitar Man", a young man leaves home to find fame and fortune as a singer. Along the way he realizes that he has lost something, and has to return to his roots to find out who he really is—"a guitar man." Elvis sings the song near the beginning of the show, and the theme is thus set. There is a gospel section and, toward the end, a long production number with song, dance, and karate, which tells the "guitar man" story. The special ended with Elvis, now wearing a white suit, singing a new song, "If I Can Dream". Written specifically for Elvis, the song was created after the writers had talked to him about his own dreams, aspirations, and fears for the future. A deeply personal song, it was a triumph for Elvis.

The show was broadcast on December 3 to massive critical and popular acclaim. It received 42 percent of the country's viewing audience and was NBC's top-rating show of the season. The soundtrack album went to No. 8 in the pop chart.

Elvis was back and he was better than ever.

OPPOSITE *Elvis performing in his black leather suit during the '68 Comeback Special.*

THE TROUBLE WITH GIRLS

Filmed in October 1968 for MGM and directed by Peter Tewksbury, who had also directed *Stay Away Joe*, *The Trouble with Girls* was about a Chautauqua, an on-the-road educational/entertainment show, and was set in the 1920s. It was an unusual movie for Elvis in that he was on screen for only about one-third of the movie, and, as the *New York Times* reviewer pointed out, it was a vehicle not so much for him but for the director. In fact, it was really an ensemble piece, and Elvis was surrounded by excellent co-stars, including John Carradine and Vincent Price.

Elvis plays Walter Hale, the manager of a visiting Chautauqua, who has to sort out the problems of his staff, which includes lecturers, musicians, and actors. The Chautauqua also becomes wrongly implicated in the murder of the local lecherous pharmacist. Walter manages to clear up the mess and win the heart of the worker's union representative, who is played by Marylyn Mason.

Despite the star cast, interesting and amusing storyline, and some pleasant songs, *The Trouble with Girls*, released on September 3, 1969, was panned by the critics and didn't do well at the box office. Only one song from the movie, "Clean Up Your Own Backyard", was released as a single.

A NOTABLE FILM

There has been a revival of interest by fans and critics in this particular Elvis film. At a time when production values on most of his films were sadly lacking, *The Trouble with Girls* stands out for being well made, with good cinematography, costumes, and sets. The ensemble cast acts well and Elvis sings some good songs, in particular "Clean Up You Own Back Yard".

CHANGE
OF HABIT

"... subdued, callow, slightly unconvincing, and largely mystified ..."

A H WEILER, THE NEW YORK TIMES, 1969

Made for NBC and Universal, this movie was the thirty-first and final feature movie in which Elvis appeared. Shooting started in March 1969 and finished in May.

It was a serious drama—though not too serious, since Elvis plays a singing doctor. Dr John Carpenter helps the needy in a deprived inner city clinic. Mary Tyler Moore plays a nun, Michelle Gallagher, who is sent to the clinic as a social worker, but who is not allowed to reveal her true vocation. Inevitably, they fall in love, and Michelle has to decide between the Church and her man. The final scene shows Michelle in church praying for guidance as to whether to remain a nun or to leave the order for Dr John. Mary Tyler Moore's character was based on a real nun, Sister Mary Oliver Gibson, who ran a speech therapy clinic in New York.

The movie was a positive experience for Elvis. He got on well with the director, William Graham, and as usual there was plenty of fun to be had with the Memphis Mafia. The director also reported that Elvis sometimes gave impromptu recitals of his hits to the cast and crew.

Only one of the movie's four songs was released to tie in with the release of the movie. "Rubberneckin", which had been recorded in Memphis, along with *From Elvis in Memphis* tracks, was the B-side to "Don't Cry Daddy".

The movie was released in November 1969 and it peaked at No. 17 on *Variety*'s weekly list. However, the *New York Times* critic A H Weiler commented that Elvis seemed "... subdued, callow, slightly unconvincing, and largely mystified ..."

ABOVE *Elvis and Mary Tyler Moore with one of Dr Carpenter's patients in* Change of Habit, *1969.*

FROM ELVIS IN MEMPHIS

From Elvis in Memphis was Elvis' comeback album. Released in June 1969, it had been recorded in January that year at the American Sound Studio in Memphis in intense sessions that sometimes ran through the night. Although it went to only No. 13 on Billboard's album chart (and to No. 3 on the country chart), many critics consider it his finest album. Essentially a country and soul album, it had all the energy of Elvis' Sun Studio recordings of the fifties, but with a new emotional intensity that simply blew away the fans and the critics. It was produced by Chips Moman and Felton Jarvis.

From his sensitive rendition of the country classic, "Gentle on My Mind", to the soulfulness of "True Love Travels on a Gravel Road", Elvis once again proved his versatility and fine touch. One outstanding track, "In the Ghetto", written by the American songwriter Mac Davis, was released as a single before the album went on sale. It reached No. 3 in the charts. The song, about a boy growing up and dying violently in the ghetto, was a controversial choice for Elvis, but the emotional power of his voice pulls it off—he was always proud of having taken it on.

The album sealed Elvis' comeback.

The Album Tracks

★ "Wearin' That Loved On Look"
★ "Only the Strong Survive"
★ "I'll Hold You in My Heart"
★ "Long Black Limousine"
★ "It Keeps Right On A-Hurtin'"
★ "I'm Moving On"
★ "Power of My Love"
★ "Gentle On My Mind"
★ "After Loving You"
★ "True Love Travels on a Gravel Road"
★ "Any Day Now"
★ "In the Ghetto"

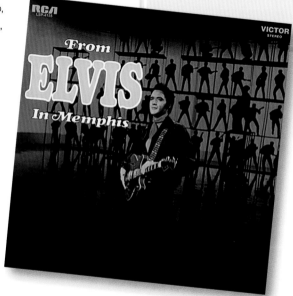

OPPOSITE *Elvis posing for a publicity photo with an acoustic guitar, around 1960.*

1969–1973
VIVA LAS VEGAS
THE NON-STOP PERFORMANCE

the International Hotel,
LAS VEGAS *1969*

"Elvis was supernatural."

DAVID DALTON, ROLLING STONE

It was as if Elvis couldn't do anything wrong. First he performed the brilliant *Comeback Show* and then the comeback album was released, and then, on July 31 at the International Hotel in Las Vegas, he gave his first live performance in eight years to a rapturous audience.

Elvis was booked for 57 performances at the International's new showroom; he would give two shows per night, one at 8 o'clock and one at midnight. Each show lasted 90 minutes. Elvis wore a karate-inspired outfit, sometimes black and sometimes white. These were designed by Bill Belew, who later fashioned Elvis' seventies one-pieces. He was very lean at this time, with longer, jet black hair.

For the first show, Elvis performed a range of hits, old and new, including "Blue Suede Shoes", "All Shook Up", "Hound Dog", "In the Ghetto", "Suspicious Minds", and "Memories". Backstage, he had been very nervous and quiet, waiting for comedian Sammy Shore to warm up the sell-out audience. Sammy Davis Jr, Juliet Prowse, Tom Jones, and Cary Grant were all there. During the show, Elvis saw Davis in the audience and, making a point of singling him out, gave him one the rings he was wearing.

Elvis bantered with the audience—who loved this new, energetic, and, most importantly, "live" Elvis. One voice of dissent was the *Las Vegas Sun* critic, who complained that the show lacked good production values. Elvis was backed by the Imperials and Sweet Inspirations, and the Bobby Moore Orchestra, but in essence it was just Elvis singing on the stage. Despite the reservations of the *Las Vegas Sun* reviewer, the audience gave Elvis a standing ovation both at the beginning and end of the

> "... I was really missing contact with a live audience ...
> and that's why I'm back. I'm really enjoying it."
>
> ELVIS, AUGUST 1 1969

show and many critics wrote ecstatic reviews. For the subsequent shows, Elvis changed some of the songs and developed more of his banter, sometimes launching into joky, almost autobiographical accounts of his life.

An emotional Elvis and Colonel Parker, both in tears, were seen embracing at the end of the first show. After the first two shows, Elvis held press conferences. On August 1, an upbeat Elvis launched an unexpected and often comic monologue about his life, laughing at his own movie career, and finished by saying: "I got into a rut in Hollywood ... I was really missing contact with a live audience ... and that's why I'm back. I'm really enjoying it." Press photos show a smiling Vernon sitting alongside Elvis.

Elvis' first live album was recorded at this concert. Called *Elvis in Person at the International Hotel*, it was the first of many. Interestingly, most tracks were recorded from the midnight shows, since Elvis generally performed better at these sessions. This was possibly because food was no longer being served to the audience or because Elvis was generally more relaxed and could extend the session if he wanted to.

After the engagement, Elvis took a break in Hawaii with Priscilla, Lisa Marie, and friends and family.

THE INTERNATIONAL HOTEL

The showroom at the International Hotel was completed in early 1969 and opened by Barbra Streisand. It became the Hilton in 1971, and Elvis performed there repeatedly during the seventies. The hotel earned around $2 million dollars for his first run in August 1969.

OPPOSITE *Elvis speaking at a press conference in Las Vegas after his July 31 performance.*

LEFT *Elvis Performing at the International Hotel in Las Vegas July 1969.*

The press conference

Foreign and domestic newsmen gathered around Elvis Presley during his August 1 press conference the day after his opening night at the International Hotel in Las Vegas, Nevada. His father, Vernon, was by his side. "I'm really glad to be back in front of a live audience," Elvis told about 150 members of the press. "I don't think I've ever been more excited than I was tonight." He performed before a star-studded crowd in the 3,000-seat International Room, his first show in public for eight years. It was also his first appearance in the hotel in more than 13 years.

SUSPICIOUS MINDS

Released on August 26, 1969, "Suspicious Minds" was Elvis' first No. 1 single in the United States for seven years. Elvis recorded the song between 4 o'clock and 7 o'clock in the morning in Memphis as part of the incredibly productive session of January 1969, where tracks for the album *From Elvis in Memphis* were laid down at the same time.

The song had first been recorded and released by its writer Mark James (who also wrote another Elvis classic, "Always on My Mind"), but it had flopped. However, Elvis loved the song, especially the version that soul producer Chips Moman introduced him to, and really wanted to do his own version.

He first sang "Suspicious Minds" at the International Hotel show in Las Vegas. One of his longest songs (four minutes and 22 seconds), it is also notable for the fadeout of nearly 15 seconds. Elvis sometimes extended it for the live performances so that it lasted for eight minutes. On stage, Elvis imbued the song with incredible emotional intensity—it became a showstopper. Above all, perhaps, the song was peculiarly apt for Elvis; his relationship with Priscilla was characterized by suspicion on both sides.

Facts

★ B-side: "You'll Think of Me"
★ Recorded: January 23, 1969
★ Released: August 26, 1969
★ Label: RCA
★ Producers: Chips Moman and Felton Jarvis
★ Writer: Mark James

OPPOSITE *Elvis performing "Suspicious Minds" in Las Vegas, 1970.*

the International Hotel,
LAS VEGAS 1970

Elvis was back in Las Vegas after Christmas 1969 for his second four-week run at the International. Some people thought it was too soon after his triumphant return in the summer, but against all expectations every seat was filled and once again Elvis received rave reviews. Stars ranging from Fats Domino to Zsa Zsa Gabor and his boyhood hero, Dean Martin, were in the audience.

In many ways, it was the same kind of show as that of 1969. Elvis' outfits were a little more flamboyant; he wore a low macramé jewel-studded belt over a white one-piece jumpsuit (a prelude to his more outrageous seventies' outfits). The songs, too, had changed. Elvis explained to the audience that he wanted to do not only his own songs, but other musicians' hits, too. Included in the repertoire in the February run were the Beatles' song "Yesterday", Joe South's "Walk A Mile in My Shoes", and Tony Joe White's "Polk Salad Annie".

Despite having a cold for the last few shows, Elvis was in good spirits throughout. He often played around during his performance, sometimes joking with the audience mid-song and intentionally changing lyrics and skipping verses to confuse the orchestra.

The show broke Elvis' own attendance records. The *Las Vegas Sun* critic called it "sheer magic throughout." The live-recorded album, *On Stage*, reached No. 13 in the Billboard album chart. A single released from the album, *The Wonder Of You*, reached No. 9 in the United States.

Facts

★ B-side: "Mama Liked The Roses"
★ Recorded Live: February 1970
★ Released: April 20, 1970
★ Label: RCA
★ Producer: Chet Atkins
★ Writer: Baker Knight

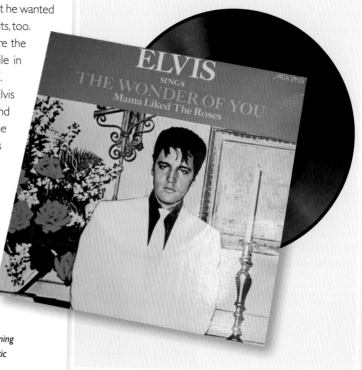

OPPOSITE *Elvis performing on stage with an acoustic guitar in 1970.*

HOUSTON ASTRODOME
Texas, 1970

The Astrodome was a huge dome that was used for a variety of functions, including rodeo shows. Following directly on from Vegas, Elvis performed just six shows here; three evening shows and three matinees. However, it was an important gig for Elvis since it was his first concert outside Vegas. The sound system and acoustics were poor, and Elvis remarked that they all just had to make the most of it. Aside from his concerns about the dome acoustics, Elvis was also worried about performing to such a large audience; the Astrodome had 44,540 seats and all were sold out. However, he was as well received as in Vegas, and was mobbed after the performance for the first time since the fifties, with fans throwing flowers at his limousine. Once again, Elvis changed the song line-up. Included in his repertoire in Texas were "Long Tall Sally", "Walk A Mile In My Shoes", "In The Ghetto", "Don't Cry Daddy", and "Kentucky Rain".

Toward the end of the run, Priscilla flew in to join Elvis. Her presence was possibly to counter stories that had appeared in the local press of a rift between the couple. After the last concert Elvis, reportedly $1.2 million richer, flew back to Los Angeles to relax and practice karate.

THE TROPHY ROOM
At a reception after the concerts, Elvis was given a handful of trophies. An RCA executive had flown in from New York to present him with five gold records, a gold deputy sheriff's badge (Elvis liked to collect them), and a Rolex watch worth $2,500. Elvis kept these in the trophy room at Graceland—a room which he set aside for his gold and platinum records and other awards.

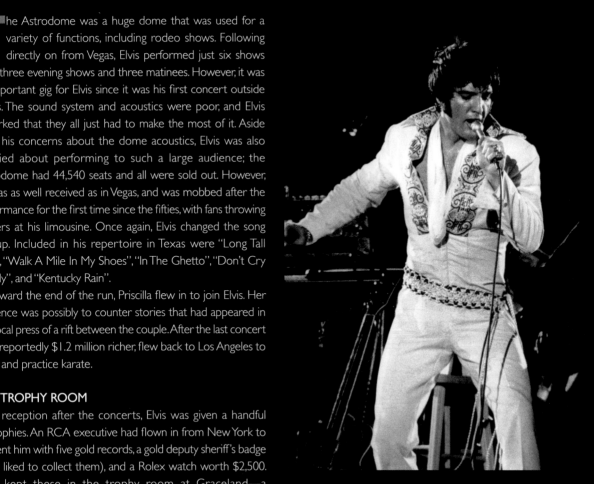

ABOVE *Elvis performing at the Houston Astrodome in 1970.*

OPPOSITE *Elvis plays guitar during a scene from the documentary movie* Elvis: That's The Way It Is, *December 1970.*

"THE ELVIS PRESLEY SUMMER FESTIVAL"

In August, Elvis was back in Las Vegas for another sell-out concert, dubbed "The Elvis Presley Summer Festival." Colonel Parker went into overdrive and the International was draped in banners and scarves, with all sorts of Elvis merchandise available. Elvis sang a large repertoire, including "Bridge Over Troubled Water", "Sweet Caroline", "Suspicious Minds", "Blue Suede Shoes", "I Just Can't Help Believin'", and "That's All Right".

Throughout the proceedings, a film crew from MGM were making a documentary about Elvis, which the Colonel had arranged. *Elvis, That's The Way* was directed by award-winning director Denis Sanders. The documentary was shot at the International and it opened in November to good reviews.

At the end of the engagement in September, a tired but exhilarated Elvis started the first of two tours that the Colonel had arranged. His first tour since 1957, it was a great success. Then, after a recording session in Nashville in November, he toured another eight cities. Again, he was warmly received and the reviews were good.

As the end of 1970 approached, Elvis was still riding high but all the professional success he was achieving seemed to come at enormous personal cost. He was hardly ever with Priscilla, pushing their already shaky marriage to the edge, and, on top of this, he had severe problems with sleep and was taking sleeping pills (in addition to many other prescription drugs) in ever-increasing quantities.

the ELVIS-NIXON SUMMIT

Much has been said about this extraordinary meeting of December 21, 1970. Initiated by Elvis, it shows just how famous he was: he turned up unexpectedly at the White House and was given a one-to-one meeting with the President. However, it also shows that Elvis was beginning to behave extremely bizarrely and develop an obsession with law enforcement and guns. He was spending hundreds of thousands of dollars buying them in large quantities and would often carry several on his person at any one time. He was now on a one-man mission to stamp out recreational drugs and their associated culture, which he believed were undermining the country.

Elvis wrote a six-page letter to Nixon on the plane to Washington. The letter, handwritten on airline stationery, declared Elvis' unease with certain elements in the country; it cited communism and the hippie culture as two of the problems. He went on to offer his services as an undercover agent to help root out such influences. Elvis presented the letter at the White House gate and, once its contents had been digested in amazement by White House staff, Elvis was led in to meet Nixon in the Oval office. Dressed in a dark cape, Elvis asked the President to make him "a federal agent at large" in the Bureau of Dangerous Drugs and Narcotics, and then, almost inexplicably, he cited the Beatles as an anti-American force. A somewhat surprised president responded by saying that he thought it was important that Elvis retain his credibility.

At the meeting, Elvis presented Nixon with a World War II Colt-45 pistol, seven silver bullets, and some family photographs. A few days later, he received a letter from Nixon thanking him for his gifts. Nixon is said to have been somewhat bemused by the meeting. The pistol in now on display at the Richard Nixon Library and Birthplace Foundation in California.

The meeting was kept secret until the *Washington Post* broke the story in January 1972. Pictures of the meeting are now the most requested item at the United States National Archives.

"a federal agent at large"

ELVIS REQUEST TO PRESIDENT NIXON, 1970

BELOW *Elvis shakes hands with President Richard Nixon in the Oval Office at the White House, 1970.*

the TEN OUTSTANDING YOUNG MEN
of the Nation

The 36-year-old Elvis started 1971 on a high note, having been named as one of the Ten Outstanding Young Men of the Nation by the United States Junior Chamber of Commerce (known as the Jaycees). The prestigious award had been given every year since 1938 to scientists, inventors, politicians, moviemakers, and entertainers. It was bestowed upon those who had contributed to the American dream of free enterprise, and who had shown patriotism and humanitarianism in their lives.

On January 16, Elvis was in Memphis for the award. The festivities were spread over the day; first there was a prayer breakfast at the Holiday Inn, Rivermont, then a luncheon, and then an evening ceremony at the Memphis Municipal Auditorium, where the award was presented. Elvis was accompanied by Priscilla and members of the Memphis Mafia. Other winners that year were cancer researcher Dr George Todara and bio-physicist Dr Mario Capecchi. Previous winners included Nelson Rockefeller, Ted Kennedy, and Howard Hughes.

Elvis, always aware that he was a poor-boy-made-good, was almost overcome and his nerves were in evidence as he began his acceptance speech. The speech lasted less than a minute but was, somehow, absolutely right for the occasion; it also quite brilliantly seemed to encapsulate Elvis, the man and the performer, in a nutshell.

ABOVE *Elvis and Sammy Davis Jr backstage after a concert in Las Vegas, 1970.*

OPPOSITE *Elvis performing for a TV special 1969.*

"When I was a child, ladies and gentlemen, I was a dreamer. I read comic books, and I was the hero of the comic book. I saw movies, and I was the hero in the movie. So every dream I ever dreamed has come true a hundred times ... I learned very early in life that 'Without a song, the day would never end; without a song, a man ain't got a friend; without a song, the road would never bend—without a song.' So I keep singing a song. Goodnight. Thank you."

ELVIS' ACCEPTANCE SPEECH, MEMPHIS, 1971

DEATH THREATS,
awards, & more concerts

In January, Elvis was back in Vegas for another month-long engagement. This one was much the same as the others: a sell out with great critical reviews; the outfits were even more flamboyant. However, this time Elvis spent much of the month genuinely terrified. He had received a death threat, which was taken seriously enough for the FBI to be called in, and he now performed under tight security and with armed bodyguards waiting in the wings.

Elvis then returned to Nashville in March for another recording session. The aim was to lay down material for a new Christmas album, *Elvis Sings The Wonderful World of Christmas*. However, after just four days, Elvis complained that his eyes hurt. The session ended prematurely and Elvis was diagnosed with glaucoma, something that would continue to plague him for the rest of his life.

In May, he went back to Nashville to complete the Christmas album and also to record a new gospel album. The resulting album, *He Touched Me*, was released in April 1972 and won Elvis his second Grammy.

In June, Elvis' birthplace in Tupelo was opened to the public and a stretch of the highway that ran past Graceland was renamed Elvis Presley Boulevard. In July, he was in Lake Tahoe for a two-week engagement, and in August was back in Vegas at the International (now the Hilton). In August, he received The Bing Crosby Award (later known as the Lifetime Achievement Award) from the National Academy of Recording Arts and Sciences. In November, he embarked on a 12-city tour.

It was a hectic schedule and the awards meant a lot to Elvis. However, when he wasn't performing he was said to be depressed, bothered by his eyes, and increasingly moody. In addition, Priscilla had begun to speak up about his use of prescription drugs.

OPPOSITE *Elvis holding his platinum record for his* As Recorded at Madison Square Garden *album.*

ABOVE *Elvis' star on the Walk of Fame in Hollywood, California.*

SEPARATION

In August 1971, Elvis and Priscilla moved into a spacious new home in the exclusive Holmby Heights area of LA. Priscilla had been in LA decorating the house for some time, while Elvis had been at Graceland. Even though the move may have looked like a new beginning for the couple, things were far from what they seemed.

Just as when she had first met him, Elvis was once again spending much of his time with his old gang. He often behaved strangely and seemed to be out of control—he was, for example, given to shooting a pistol just to attract attention. Worst of all for Priscilla were the other women, and she suspected correctly that Elvis brought girlfriends back to Graceland while she was at their LA home.

But Priscilla had a secret of her own. She was having an affair with Mike Stone, her karate instructor. Ironically, she had taken up karate to share Elvis' passion, and had taken it seriously, quickly becoming accomplished in the art.

By Christmas 1971, the façade was beginning to slip. At the festivities, guests could sense the distance between the couple. Finally, just before the New Year, Priscilla left with Lisa Marie and returned to California to be with Stone. At first Elvis didn't seem to accept the seriousness of the situation, but once he was aware of Priscilla's affair and realized that she wasn't coming back, he was devastated. For a time, he talked about killing Mike Stone but later dropped the idea. No matter how unfaithful he had been, he had expected Priscilla to be true to him and had assumed that they would always remain husband and wife. Despite everything he had done, he believed the institution of marriage to be sacred.

RIGHT *Elvis and Priscilla with Vernon Presley in late 1970.*

ELVIS ON TOUR

In January 1972, Elvis was back in Vegas for another engagement at the Hilton. For these concerts, he added a full-length cape to his costume, as well as a new song, "An American Trilogy". The latter was, in fact, three Civil War songs, "Dixie", "The Battle Hymn of the Republic", and "All My Trials", which had been pieced together and made into a Top 40 hit by singer Mickey Newbury in 1971. Elvis loved performing this song and it became one of his concert classics. However, troubled by Priscilla's departure, Elvis performed erratically, earning himself both good and bad reviews from the critics, although as far as his fans were concerned it seemed that he could do no wrong.

When the run finished, Elvis went to MGM in Culver City to meet two moviemakers, Pierre Adidge and Robert Abel, who were interested in producing a second documentary about his life. It would follow him on his next tour, which was set to begin in April and would encompass 15 cities. The movie aimed to give a more complete picture of the man and his music than ever before, with rehearsals, concerts, and behind-the-scenes action. To Elvis' delight, the resulting movie, *Elvis on Tour*, won a Golden Globe for Best Documentary in 1973.

HE TOUCHED ME

In April 1972, the gospel album that Elvis had recorded in Nashville in May 1971 was released to great acclaim. At a time when most of Elvis' studio recordings didn't stand out critically, *He Touched Me* was a breath of fresh air. The album won Elvis his second Grammy for Best Inspirational Album and sold over one million copies in the United States. Tracks include "He Touched Me", "Amazing Grace", "Reach Out To Jesus", and "A Thing Called Love".

OPPOSITE AND RIGHT *Elvis on stage during his 1972 Las Vegas Hilton Performance.*

the MADISON SQUARE GARDEN
concert

Q: Elvis, are you satisfied with your image?

A: Well, sir, it's very hard to live up to an image.

(MADISON SQUARE GARDEN PRESS CONFERENCE, JUNE 1972)

In June, to begin a new 12-day tour, Elvis played four sell-out concerts in the Madison Square Garden arena in New York. It was an important test for Elvis—he had never played a concert to a New York audience before; his last New York experience had been in 1956 on the *Ed Sullivan Show*, when he had received widespread criticism. As a result, both the Colonel and Elvis were nervous. Once again, they needn't have worried. In a white jewel-encrusted jumpsuit, Elvis dazzled New York, receiving rave views for his showmanship and charisma. He sang 20 numbers, mostly his old hits, plus a few new songs, notably "Never Been To Spain", "For the Good Times", and "The Impossible Dream". He received stupendous applause throughout. The New York concert had begun with a press conference on June 9. Elvis was in a jocular mood and entered the conference room saying: "I'm innocent of all charges." When asked how he'd outlasted every other performer from his generation, he laughed and said "I take vitamin E." When asked about his "humbleness" he said "yes" he was "shy" and then stood up to show off his solid gold belt buckle—a gift from the International Hotel. The Colonel then wound up proceedings and Elvis left the stage with the Colonel and his father to cheers and applause from the assembled journalists.

In July, when the tour had finished and Elvis was back in Memphis, he and Priscilla formally separated. By this time, he had a new love: Linda Thompson, a 22-year old Memphis beauty queen, who was to be his companion for four years.

ABOVE *Elvis on tour, April 1972*

OPPOSITE *Elvis laughs and chats to journalists at the Madison Square Garden press conference.*

BURNING LOVE

Elvis recorded "Burning Love" in March 1972 in Hollywood at a session where little else was achieved. It was released in August of that year and rose to No. 2 on the Billboard Hot 100 Chart in the United States. It was to be Elvis' last top ten hit in the United States. "Burning Love" was certified gold in October 1972 and went platinum in March 1973.

It was one of the few rock songs recorded by Elvis in the seventies. He hadn't wanted to record it and had to be persuaded by the session musicians and the producer Felton Jarvis in the studio. He was singing mostly ballads at the time, and, after his separation from Priscilla, didn't seem in the mood for a rock 'n' roll number. However, when he finally took it on, it took only six takes to get it right. Interestingly, at a time when he was singing emotive ballads and belting out anthems such as "American Trilogy", Elvis takes an almost mellow approach to this number.

"Burning Love" never became a classic Elvis hit, and he himself never seemed to have really taken to it and rarely sang it at his concerts, but despite this, the song has maintained an enduring appeal. The line "hunka hunka burning love" has been endlessly parodied by Elvis impersonators.

OPPOSITE *Elvis during a press conference for the January 1973* Aloha From Hawaii *special.*

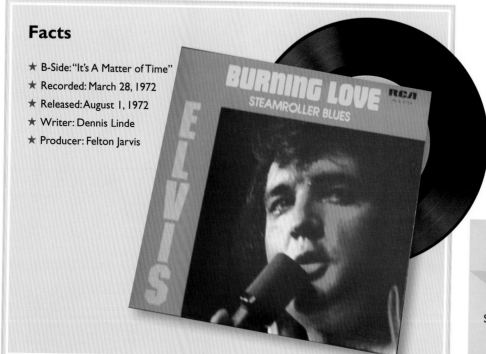

Facts

★ B-Side: "It's A Matter of Time"
★ Recorded: March 28, 1972
★ Released: August 1, 1972
★ Writer: Dennis Linde
★ Producer: Felton Jarvis

Did You Know?

Elvis' "Burning Love" was used on the 2008 space shuttle mission STS-123 as the wake-up song on Day 10.

ALOHA *from* HAWAII

This television show broke many records and made one significant first. It was the first show to be broadcast by satellite across the world. It is a tribute to Elvis' unique place in the hearts and minds of his fans that he was chosen to be the first entertainer to be seen live worldwide.

The Aloha concerts took place on January 12 and 14, 1973, at the Honolulu International Center Arena; the January 14 show was beamed live to Australia, South Korea, Japan, Thailand, and the Philippines, as well as European countries, where it was seen with a slight time delay. In the United States, it was broadcast on April 4 and was watched by 51 percent of the TV viewing audience. Approximately 1.1 billion people worldwide viewed Aloha. An astounding 91 percent of the population of viewers in the Philippines saw it. The live album went to No.1 on the United States Billboard Pop Album chart.

Elvis commissioned his costume designer, Bill Belew, to create an American Eagle for his jumpsuit. The eagle was to represent America—Elvis was nothing if not patriotic. Before the show he had been asked by the producer to lose weight, which he did using a combination of vitamin injections, crash diets, and strenuous karate workouts.

Elvis sang a mix of his old hits, and many of the ballads that he now preferred: "My Way", "Suspicious Minds", "I'm so Lonesome I Could Cry" (a Hank Williams number), and the Beatles' "Something" were in the repertoire. Once again, Elvis showed his vocal range, but there were those who felt that some of the edge and passion were now missing. If he sometimes had a faraway look in his eyes, it may have been because he was in the process of divorcing Priscilla.

The two concerts were performed for charity. For the first concert, the tickets had no price. Each audience member was asked to donate what they could, raising an estimated $75,000 The proceeds went to the Kui Lee Cancer Fund in Hawaii. Kui Lee was a young Hawaiian songwriter who had died of cancer.

OPPOSITE *Elvis singing in his "Aloha Eagle" jumpsuit during a concert in Honolulu, Hawaii, January 1973.*

ABOVE *Elvis at the International Convention Center Arena, Honolulu, Hawaii, January 1973.*

the SHOW GOES ON

After the spectacle of Aloha, Elvis was back at the Hilton in Vegas for another engagement in February. Despite the Aloha success, he seemed depressed and immediately put on weight. His health was suffering, too; the cocktail of drugs (pain killers, amphetamines, and sleeping pills) was finally taking its toll. During the engagement, his throat and lungs became severely inflamed, most likely as a result of the drugs, and, for the first time ever, he was forced to cancel several performances.

On March 1, Colonel Parker sold all the rights to Elvis' records to date to RCA. A brilliant deal for the Colonel, who received a large one-off payment, but it meant that neither Elvis nor his family would ever receive record royalties. As well as this, Elvis and the Colonel signed a new deal in which they were 50–50 partners. In late April, Elvis went on an eight-city tour; in May there was an engagement at Lake Tahoe, and in June another tour; then back to the Hilton.

The concerts were still sellouts but Elvis looked bloated and in ill health, and critics began to comment on the unevenness of the shows and his changed appearance.

Throughout all of this, Linda Thompson was at his side. Overnight it was as if she had become his nurse. A few years later, she left Elvis, saying she couldn't wait around to see him self-destruct.

On October 9, Elvis and Priscilla were in court in Santa Monica to finalize their divorce. Pictures show them leaving arm in arm; Elvis is looking bloated in a tracksuit, while Priscilla outwardly looks calm. She said later that she was worried and surprised by the change in his appearance. The divorce was amicable and they both shared custody of Lisa Marie, although it was arranged that she would live with her mother.

RIGHT *Linda Thompson at the Philadelphia Hilton Hotel, 1974.*

OPPOSITE *Elvis and Priscilla leaving court together after their divorce hearing, October 1973.*

the MEMPHIS MAFIA

OPPOSITE *Elvis and the "Memphis Mafia" at the wedding of his bodyguard Sonny West, December 1970.*

BELOW *Elvis with Sonny West, on his wedding day.*

Elvis may have often felt lonely, but he was rarely alone. From his days in the army, he surrounded himself with a bunch of male friends, who were also on his payroll, sharing his homes, holidays, and parties. They acted as bodyguards and assistants, and generally protected him from the press and public. They accompanied him on movie shoots and recording sessions; their presence meant that few outsiders could ever really get to know Elvis.

Nearly all were from Memphis (hence the Memphis Mafia) and some, such as Red West, had been at high school with him. Others, such as Jo Esposito and Charlie Hodge, had met Elvis in the army, and others were relatives, including Gene and Junior Smith, who were cousins. Over the years the faces changed, although some, such as Red West and Jo Esposito, were always part of Elvis' life.

To some extent, the Memphis Mafia were enjoying a gravy train, accepting Elvis' extraordinary generosity, which included regular bonuses and gifts of cars and houses. In return, they had to put up with his moods and jibes, his bizarre actions, and, by the seventies, his drug use. They also had to accept that they would never be thought of or treated as equals. When lifelong friend Red West was summarily fired in 1976 for being too heavy-handed with the public, he was devastated by Elvis' coldness. Red went on to write, along with his cousin Sonny West and Dave Hebler, *Elvis, What Happened*. Known as The Bodyguard Book, it was an expose of Elvis' drug taking and its intention was partly to bring Elvis to his senses. Published in 1977, it was, however, too late.

1973–1977
THE LATER YEARS

IN CONCERT
1973–1974

A week after the divorce hearing, Elvis was rushed to hospital in Memphis in a semi-comatose condition. He was diagnosed with pneumonia, pleurisy, hepatitis, and an enlarged colon. His girlfriend, Linda Thompson, was at his bedside for the two weeks during which he was hospitalized. She was now living with him at Graceland.

His personal physician, Dr George Nichopoulos, known as Dr Nick, put the illness down to a cocktail of drugs Elvis had been given in LA by a doctor who didn't know about his other medication. Whatever the exact reason, the problems were a result of his excessive use of prescription drugs. Elvis, however, was in complete denial and simply wouldn't listen to anyone who questioned his drug taking. From this point onward Elvis' health declined, and drug-related illness and cancelled concerts became part of his life. His concerts were still well received by his fans, but he became as well known for his rambling monologues and frolicking about on stage as for his music.

LEFT *Elvis performing in 1974.*

Following the illness, Dr Nick insisted that Elvis rest at Graceland, and, with Linda at his side, he took the health scare seriously enough to slow down for the rest of the year. His next live engagement was at the Hilton, in January 1974.

VEGAS 1974

On Dr Nick's orders, the month-long engagement starting in January was cut to two weeks. When it ended, Elvis was back on the road touring. The shows received varying reviews. Some critics felt that Elvis was bored and rushing through songs and shows.

In September, he was back in Vegas, but by now the fans and press knew something was seriously wrong. At a concert on September 2, 1974, Elvis launched into a tirade on stage, denying reports that he was "strung out" on heroin. The only thing he'd ever been "strung out on," Elvis insisted, was music. The audience began by applauding him and laughing but, as his anger mounted, the cheers and applause weakened. Despite this, the fans continued to give him standing ovations, and there were still songs that Elvis could work wonders with. He poured emotion into his ballads and, even when rambling through old stories, he retained his magnetic stage presence.

In Vegas, Elvis was made an offer that could possibly have turned all of this around. Barbra Streisand approached him to ask if he would co-star alongside her in a remake of the movie *A Star is Born*. Elvis was keen, but once again the Colonel intervened. He asked for too much money and demanded that his star be given equal billing with Streisand. The producers refused, and the part eventually went to Kris Kristofferson.

After Vegas, Elvis went back on tour. He had put on weight and looked terrible. He hurried through shows and some were cut short. Despite this, tickets still sold like hot cakes. After the tour, Elvis took a break for several months. He planned and became quite excited about a karate movie he hoped to make either a documentary or an action feature movie. Unfortunately, due to his recurring poor health, the movie was never made.

In January 1975 Elvis turned 40; the press reported that he was 40 and fat. By the end of January, he was back in hospital.

Colonel Parker:
PUSHING *his* STAR *to the* LIMIT

One of the mysteries of Elvis' career is why he gave so much power to just one man—the Colonel. And, why did the Colonel, at a time when his star obviously needed help, push him so hard with an endless round of engagements and exhausting tours?

One reason was money. Although Elvis was the highest-paid entertainer of his day, he had no regard for money and spent lavishly. The Colonel, too, had an expensive lifestyle. While Elvis spent money on drugs, expensive gifts, guns, cars, and houses, the Colonel spent his on gambling. No one knows exactly how much he lost at the Las Vegas casino tables, but it was in the region of many millions of dollars.

Another more benign explanation put forward by some is that the Colonel thought it was better for Elvis to work—he may have believed that not working would cause the star to have a complete breakdown. Another theory is that he didn't really know how to handle an incredibly famous star, and just did what he knew best: organizing tours and concerts.

It was the Colonel who made Elvis do the endless round of movies; who prevented his possible comeback with *A Star Is Born*. It was the Colonel who persuaded him to sign away a large amount of his royalties from RCA for a single payment. It was the Colonel who refused to allow Elvis to tour in Europe, something he wanted to do—Parker said it was too much a of a security risk, but the fact was, as an illegal immigrant, the Colonel didn't have a passport.

But it was also the Colonel who had made Elvis. His brilliant handling of the young singer, getting him on the top TV shows of the time and the way he dealt with the army years, are a part of what made what made Elvis such a huge phenomenon. Elvis himself believed so. "I don't think I would have been big with another man," he once said of the Colonel, "because he's a very smart man."

ABOVE *Elvis with Colonel Tom Parker, around 1956.*

Colonel Parker

Ⓞne of the constants in Elvis' life, Colonel Tom Parker engineered Elvis' career from his days on the Louisiana Hayride. In the main picture, backstage before Elvis' second appearance on the *Ed Sullivan Show* in 1956, Ed Sullivan explains something to Colonel Tom Parker as Elvis looks on.

The Colonel was also instrumental in getting Elvis into movies and, taken in around 1969, the picture below shows Elvis Presley conferring with him on the set of a movie.

CONCERTS & RECORDINGS
1975–1976

In March 1975, Elvis was back at the Hilton and in April he was on tour again. After one concert in July, Elvis bought his entire 14-member band a Cadillac each. This year he would also buy himself two airplanes. In August he was back in Vegas, but he had to end his engagement early and was hospitalized in Memphis. During one performance, he had been so tired he had to sit down on stage. The press reported that he was suffering from fatigue, possibly brought on by a crash diet. The reporter from the *Las Vegas Sun* noted that it was the fifth time he had canceled a concert since 1973.

In November 1975, he was back in Vegas. In January, he took a break in Colorado. He was back on tour again in March. The tours continued throughout 1976, with more and more stage antics and some great performances, too. At a recording session in the den at Graceland in February, Elvis laid down several tracks for his next country album, *From Elvis Presley Boulevard, Memphis, Tennessee*, which went to No. 1 in the country chart in May and eventually went gold. On July 5, Elvis gave his last concert in Memphis.

"WAY DOWN"

In October 1976, Elvis was back recording in the den at Graceland. This time he recorded "Way Down", which was released in June 1977, his last single released during his lifetime. It went to No. 18 in the singles pop chart. After his death, it went to No. 1 in the United States. Written by Laying Martine Jr, it was later a hit for Status Quo. Despite his problems, this recording shows that Elvis' voice could still hit the mark.

In November 1976, Elvis and Linda Thompson split up.

ABOVE *Elvis on his way to perform at Nassau Coliseum, July 19, 1975.*

OPPOSITE *Elvis performs on stage on July 23, 1975 in Asheville, North Carolina.*

Ginger Alden:

ELVIS' LAST LOVE

In late November 1976, Elvis met Ginger Alden. Ginger was just 20 years old and, like Linda, a Memphis beauty queen. Elvis had just split up from Linda—she had been unable to deal with his drug-taking and self-destructive tendencies. Also, as she must have known, there had been other women throughout the relationship. The actress Cybill Shepherd, another Memphis beauty queen, was one of them. Elvis met her in 1972 when she was 27.

Ginger was young, shy, and very naïve. Elvis seemed to adore her right from the beginning. At their first meeting, he talked to her about religion, read spiritual texts, and sang to her. He told his friends that he had found the one he wanted to be with and tried to spend all his time with her. He showered her with gifts; the first was a white Lincoln Mark 4. To begin with, she seemed to lift his mood and his friends thought that maybe things were turning for the better. He took her on tour with him but, on one occasion, when she missed her family, he reluctantly let her return to them; another time he flew her family out on his private jet to join them at his concert. When her grandfather died, Elvis flew her whole family to the funeral in Arkansas. He seemed desperate to please her.

On January 26, 1977, Elvis proposed to Ginger, giving her an 11.5-carat diamond ring. He introduced her to his concert audiences as his girlfriend. He was clearly infatuated with her, if not truly in love.

LEFT *Elvis with girlfriend Linda Thompson at the Hilton Hotel in Cincinnati, Ohio, March 1976.*

OPPOSITE *Elvis with his girlfriend Ginger Alden in March 1977 in Hawaii.*

the LAST LAS VEGAS GIG

On November 30, 1976, Elvis gave a concert at Anaheim, California; John Wayne was in the audience. In December, Elvis was back at The Hilton in Vegas, for what would be his last concert there. Infatuated with Ginger, he was in good spirits, if a little distracted by her from the business in hand. Once again, there wasn't a spare seat in the house.

Elvis opened well but, as the shows continued, he seemed more and more fatigued. He was also overweight and didn't move well on stage. At one show he appeared to be drunk (Priscilla and Lisa Marie were in the audience for this performance); at another he made several false starts to several songs; at another he had to ask for the lyrics to a particular song. At yet another show, he complained that his throat was dry "like the Mojave Desert." Throughout he looked pale and bloated.

The shows varied from good, to poor, to disturbing. Elvis sang from an extensive repertoire and took requests from the audience. Included were "Hurt", "Love Letters", "Reconsider Baby", "Bridge Over Troubled Water", and "Danny Boy".

There were many stressful situations for Elvis during this engagement. He hurt his ankle (possibly spraining it). At one show Priscilla's parents were in the audience (Elvis dedicated "My Way" to them); Ginger's parents attended another. Then Vernon was taken to hospital with a suspected heart attack—it turned out to be just a scare and he recovered quickly—but, all in all, what had started out on a positive note for Elvis had quickly become a strenuous undertaking.

Reviews from fans and critics were mixed. It was Elvis' last performance at the Hilton.

OPPOSITE AND RIGHT *Elvis performing in 1975.*

NEW YEAR'S EVE *in Pittsburgh*

The one true concert highlight of the year was Elvis' performance in Pittsburgh at the Civic Center Arena on New Year's Eve, 1976. Elvis appeared to be in good form: relaxed, entertaining, and enthusiastic. He was on stage for the full 90 minutes and, the critics agreed, in great voice. He gave out scarves, interacted charmingly with the fans, and sang "Jailhouse Rock", "Unchained Melody", "Fever", "Little Sister", and other numbers to tumultuous applause. He surprised the audience (and the band) when he sang a Tony Bennett hit "Rags to Riches", which had obviously not been rehearsed. The audience loved it. He left the stage about half an hour before midnight, and returned at midnight to sing "Auld Lang Syne".

Despite the fact that the star was in poor health, overweight, and unfit, it was clear that the fans loved him. It was the last good concert that Elvis gave. The *Pittsburgh Post Gazette* praised his vocal ability and his "iron grip" on the enraptured audience. The

> ### "... you can grow old as a country singer but not as a rock singer ..."
>
> THE *PITTSBURGH POST GAZETTE*, 1976

critic also noted, however, that: "A famous country artist once said that you can grow old as a country singer but not as a rock singer; Presley is trying to prove him wrong. But he's not succeeding."

The success of Pittsburgh, stood out sharply against events at the beginning of 1977. Elvis was scheduled to record in Nashville in early January, but after flying there he went to his hotel room, keeping the musicians waiting in the studio, only to fly back to Memphis a few days later. He had asked Ginger to accompany him to Nashville but she had refused.

RIGHT *RCA recording studio in Nashville, Tennessee.*

CONCERTS & CANCELLATIONS

From February 12–21, Elvis was touring. He played ten concerts in the South, starting in Florida. He was a little overweight but seemed well. Once again, his performances were variable. Some songs were well under par, but he could still win over the audience—though, on one occasion, he remonstrated with them for their poor response.

At the end of the tour, Elvis was exhausted and arranged a trip to Hawaii with Ginger and some friends. He stayed in a beach house at Kailua on Oahau. The break proved a success; Elvis managed to relax, have some fun, and enjoyed playing touch football. The fun was cut short, however, when he scratched his cornea, and the group returned to Memphis early.

A new 12-show tour was scheduled to start in late March, but four of the shows were canceled due to Elvis' ill health. At one concert, in Alexandria, Louisiana, on March 30, Elvis ended the concert with the seemingly prophetic lines, "Wise men know, when it's time to go", from "Can't Help Falling In Love". Elvis became ill once again after this concert. The next four shows were canceled and Elvis returned to Memphis, where he was admitted to hospital; after being given medication he slept for 30 hours.

Almost as soon as he had recovered, he was back on tour in late April. In Chicago, on May 2, Elvis told the fans that, "In spite of everything you've heard, I'm in good health and happy to be here."

The concerts were still sellouts, but both fans and critics felt they were being short-changed. The reviewer from the *Milwaukee Journal* titled his review of the April 28 concert, "Fans of Elvis Pay A Lot To See A Little."

RIGHT *Elvis in the 1970 movie* **That's The Way It Is.**

Last concerts

In one of his last concerts, an exhausted looking Elvis Presley performs in his trademark jumpsuit on stage at the Municipal Auditorium in Austin, Texas on March 28, 1977 (see below and right).

The main picture shows Elvis being escorted into a car, 1977.

FINAL
TOURS *1977*

Elvis' penultimate tour began on May 20 and ended on June 2. CBS were scheduled to make a special, *Elvis in Concert*, and filmed several of the shows. On May 29, at a concert in Baltimore, Elvis was so weak that he had to leave the show for more than 20 minutes after the first half hour. His loyal backing artists, including the Sweet Inspirations, did their best to keep the audience happy, and Elvis later returned to finish the show, but some fans asked for a refund.

The final tour began in Springfield, Missouri, on June 17. The concerts were pretty poor throughout, despite some good reviews. On June 22, the *Sioux Falls Argus* reported: "When he sang, he was Elvis the king again. With a voice as distinctive as has ever blistered a concert hall." For most shows, however, Elvis' banter had dwindled to almost non-comprehensible murmurings, he kept having to restart songs, he sometimes didn't finish them, and he often looked physically unstable on stage. The CBS special, *Elvis in Concert*, was filmed mainly at the concert in Rapid City, South Dakota. Remarkably, Elvis looked slimmer and was in better voice. This may have been the result of taking antidepressants and going on one of his crash diets in order to look good for the cameras. Nevertheless, released after his death on October 3, the show witnessed Elvis' decline and shocked many viewers.

OPPOSITE *A live shot from a performance in 1976.*

the BACKING GROUPS

THE SEVENTIES' BACKING GROUPS

Elvis' backing groups and singers in the seventies were integral to his studio sound as well as to his live shows. By the mid-sixties, he was being backed by the Imperials, who were in the studio for his first non-soundtrack recording sessions in 1966. Out of these sessions came the award-winning gospel album *How Great Thou Art*. The Imperials worked with Elvis for the next five years, both in the studio and on stage, and featured in the documentary *Elvis: That's the Way It Is* in 1970. When the Imperials left in the early seventies, Elvis needed a new backing group. He was delighted to get JD Sumner and the Stamps Quartet.

JD Sumner had sung with the Blackwood Brothers in the sixties. The Blackwood Brothers were gospel heroes of Elvis and, growing up in Memphis, he had often listened to them at the Ellis Auditorium. The Stamps and JD Sumner worked with Elvis through the seventies, in studio and on stage. They can be seen on the film *Elvis On Tour*.

THE SWEET INSPIRATIONS

Along with JD Sumner and the Stamps Quartet, the female group the Sweet Inspirations often opened Elvis' concerts in the seventies. Both groups would perform their own songs at the beginning of the show. Although the Sweet Inspirations appeared with Elvis on almost all his concert tours, including his final tour, they never recorded with him in the studio. They can be seen in *Elvis: That's The Way It Is* and *Elvis On Tour*. One member of the quartet was Cissy Houston, Whitney Houston's mother.

"THE LITTLE GIRL WITH THE BEAUTIFUL HIGH VOICE"

Classically trained soprano Kathy Westmoreland backed Elvis on stage and on recordings from 1970 to 1977. When introducing his band and singers on stage, Elvis would point to Kathy and describe her as "the little girl with the beautiful high voice."

LEFT *The Sweet Inspirations performing on stage, around 1970.*

ABOVE *The Sweet Inspirations.*

the LAST CONCERT

The concert at the Market Square Arena in Indianapolis, Indiana, on June 26 was possibly the best of the 1977 tours. The audience numbered about 18,000 and Elvis sang for the full 90 minutes, which was, by this time, unusual. He wore a gold and white jumpsuit and white boots, and seemed to have more energy than in previous shows. He did the usual numbers, and three relatively unusual ones: "Bridge Over Troubled Water", "Release Me", and "I Can't Stop Loving You".

At one point, Elvis introduced his father, Ginger and her parents, some cousins, his doctor, and Felton Jarvis, all of whom were in the audience. He invited his father up on stage and Vernon gave a wave to the audience. The audience lapped up the performance but backstage, afterward, Elvis was said to have looked unusually tired.

After the concert, he returned to Graceland to relax in preparation for his next tour in August.

MOODY BLUE

A month after this concert, Elvis was in Memphis when his album *Moody Blue* was released on July 19. It received good reviews and sold well. The album was a mixture of live and studio work. Most of the studio sessions had been recorded in 1976. It became a Top 40 hit during his lifetime, and soared to No. 3 after his death. One of the highlights of the album is his version of "Unchained Melody", which was recorded at the concert in Ann Arbor, Michigan, in April 1977. He performed "Unchained Melody" at the piano at many of his last concert performances—right up to the end of his life, he invested incredible emotion in this particular song. Early editions of the album were pressed in blue vinyl to reflect the title track.

The Album Tracks

★ "Unchained Melody"

★ "If You Love Me (Let Me Know)"

★ "Little Darlin'"

★ "He'll Have to Go"

★ "Let Me Be There"

★ "Way Down"

★ "Pledging My Love"

★ "Moody Blue"

★ "She Thinks I Still Care"

★ "It's Easy For You"

" 'Til we meet you again, may God bless you. Adios."

ELVIS, JUNE 1977

ABOVE *Elvis performing in Lincoln,
Nebraska on June 20, 1977.*

THE END OF AN ERA

lvis spent July in almost total seclusion in his bedroom suite at Graceland. He saw a few old friends, played the occasional game of racketball, and read his spiritual books. He was upset by the imminent publication of *Elvis, What Happened*, written by his old friends Red and Sonny West and David Hebler. The Wests and Hebler had been fired by Elvis a year earlier, and had written an exposé of the star's lifestyle and drug use. The book was published at the end of July and the press picked up on it immediately. Around the world, salacious stories about Elvis were now in circulation.

In August, Lisa Marie came to stay for two weeks. Though Elvis saw her every day, he mainly left it to Ginger and others in the household to play with her.

On Monday, August 15, late at night, Elvis went to his dentist with Ginger and had a cap fitted. On Tuesday, August 16 he played racketball in the early hours of the morning and then went to bed. At 9 o'clock in the morning, Ginger woke to find Elvis reading in bed. He said he couldn't sleep and would continue reading in the bathroom. It is thought that at this point he may have taken some of the many drugs that were in his bathroom cabinet. When Ginger woke again at 2 o'clock in the afternoon, Elvis was not beside her. She called out to him and, when he didn't answer, opened the bathroom door. Elvis was lying slumped on the floor.

Ginger called for help and various people staying at Graceland, including Vernon, rushed into the room. Attempts were made to resuscitate Elvis, while Ginger kept Lisa Marie away from the bathroom. The star was rushed to hospital where more attempts at resuscitation were made. Thirty minutes after arriving at hospital, Elvis was pronounced dead.

The cause of death was given as cardiac arrhythmia—a heart attack. Elvis was 42.

OPPOSITE *Lisa Marie Presley at nine years old in March 1977.*

BELOW *Graceland, decked with flowers, was where Elvis' body was viewed by hundreds of his fans.*

THE FINAL CURTAIN

Elvis' body lay in an open casket at Graceland while thousands of fans filed by. Every bouquet in Memphis sold out. Tributes from politicians and musicians poured in. The National Guard stood by the gates of Graceland, where an estimated 75,000 people gathered.

Priscilla, Lisa Marie, and the Colonel were at the funeral. The Colonel wore shorts and an open-necked shirt. Linda Thompson and Ginger were there, too. The only celebrity ex-girlfriend who was present was an openly weeping Ann-Margret. Vernon was completely distraught.

A cavalcade of 14 white Cadillacs and a hearse drove Elvis' body to Forest Hill Cemetery, where Elvis' mother had previously been laid to rest.

The day after the funeral 50,000 fans visited his grave. Everybody, except close friends, associates, and family, seemed stunned. Elvis was really dead.

The *Memphis Press Scimitar* announced "Lonely Life Ends on Elvis Presley Boulevard." In Tupelo, the mayor declared August 16 an official day of mourning.

Lisa Marie was made the main beneficiary to Elvis' estate and Vernon was to administer the estate during his lifetime. In the event, he died just two years' later—some say from a broken heart.

Elvis and his mother were later reburied in the Meditation Garden at Graceland. The Meditation Garden was also Vernon's final resting place and that of Elvis' paternal grandmother.

BELOW *Elvis' hearse being driven down the Graceland driveway during his funeral.*

OPPOSITE *Elvis' grave in the Meditation Garden at Graceland.*

"Elvis Presley's death deprives our country of a part of itself. He was unique, irreplaceable. More than twenty years ago, he burst upon the scene with an impact that was unprecedented and will probably never be equaled. His music and his personality, fusing the styles of white country and black rhythm and blues, permanently changed the face of American popular culture. His following was immense. And he was a symbol to people the world over of the vitality, rebelliousness, and good humor of this country."

President Jimmy Carter, official statement following Elvis' death, 1977

The funeral

Thousands of people stand on the sidewalk and in the street in Memphis, Tennessee, to watch the funeral procession of Elvis Presley on August 18, 1977 (see main picture).

The front of Graceland is swamped by floral tributes (see right).

Below, mourners watch as pallbearers carry the coffin into his mausoleum at Graceland.

Dr Nick & the prescription
MEDICATION

While the cause of Elvis' death was officially a heart attack, later tests showed that there were more than 14 prescription drugs—some at levels way above their safe dosage—in his system.

Many doctors supplied Elvis with prescription medication, but one in particular, Dr Nichopoulos, was later singled out for criticism. Dr Nick was Elvis' personal physician from 1967 until Elvis' death in 1977. Elvis first asked for his help in treating his insomnia. Dr Nick had had a successful and well-respected practice in Memphis before becoming Elvis' physician. In 1980 he was brought before the Medical Board Tribunal on charges of overprescribing drugs to Elvis and Jerry Lee Lewis and 12 other patients. In 1977 alone, Dr Nick had prescribed more than 10,000 doses of uppers, downers, diet pills, antidepressants, and other drugs to Elvis. The board found him guilty of overprescribing but not that he had acted unethically. The district attorney also looked into whether Dr Nick could be charged with murdering Elvis, but because there was some medical dispute over the cause of Elvis' death, no charges were brought. In 1995, however, Dr Nick was found to have been overprescribing to patients for many years and was disqualified.

Elvis had started to take amphetamines in the army; before Dr Nick became his physician, he sent friends and associates to buy drugs for him. Dr Nick has said that he tried to control and regulate the star's intake. As well as prescribing drugs for Elvis, he had also prescribed thousands of placebos to try to wean his patient off the real drugs. Opinion is still divided on the role Dr Nick played in Elvis' tragic death.

RIGHT *Elvis' former girlfriend, Ginger Alden, outside the courtroom where Dr Nick was under investigation.*

OPPOSITE *Elvis playing guitar, around 1958.*

Index

Index

References

The text was written with reference to taped interviews given by Elvis Presley, his movies and records. The following books and websites were also used as sources.

Books

Last Train to Memphis
Peter Guralnick
Little Brown and Company, 1994.

Careless Love
Peter Guralnick
Little Brown and Company, 1999.
Together these books form the definitive biography of Elvis.

Elvis and Gladys
Elaine Dundy
Macmillan, 1985.
A detailed and unique insight into the mother and son relationship.

Elvis, The Biography
Jerry Hopkins
Plexus Publishing Ltd, 2007.
An updated account of Elvis by one of his first biographers.

The Rough Guide To Elvis
Paul Simpson
Rough Guides Ltd, 2004.
A biography, and lots of album, single, and movie reviews.

Elvis and Me
Priscilla Presley with Sandra Harmon
Berkley, 1986.
Personal reminiscences of Elvis' wife.

Websites

www.elvis.com
The official Elvis Presley website

www.elvis.com.au and
www.elvispreselymusic.com.au
The websites of the official Australian fan club, packed with biographical information, interviews, and reviews.

www.girlsguidetoelvis.com
A fun website that looks at his clothes, girl-friends, movies, and more.

www.elvispresleynews.com
Lots of news, interviews, and photos

In addition, the author would like to acknowledge reference to the following websites:
www.scottmoore.net
www.vegas.com
www.humeshighclassof53.com
www.theofficialcharts.com
www.geocities.com/elvismdb

Acknowledgments

Picture Credits

The publisher would like to thank the following for permission to reproduce the following copyright material:

Albertson, Jeff/CORBIS: 181; Bettmann/CORBIS: Front cover, 1, 21, 24, 33, 34, 39, 51, 52, 54, 56, 66, 72, 76, 80, 81, 82, 83, 92, 94, 98, 101, 110, 112, 113, 115, 119, 123, 125, 126, 132, 135, 137, 147, 148b, 160, 161, 168, 169, 180, 183, 187, 190, 192, 206, 211, 213, 216b, 217, 218; Bibikow, Walter/JAI/CORBIS: Brooks Kraft/Sygma/CORBIS: Carroll, Frank/Sygma/CORBIS: 148t, 153, 188 and 189; CBS Photo Archive/Getty Images Entertainment: 194; CBS Photo Archive/Hulton Archive/Getty: 53t and 207; Content Mine International/Alamy: 117, 136, 143 and 203; CORBIS: 83 and 193; Cravens, Don /Time & Life Pictures/Getty: 32, 65, 69; Diltz, Henry/CORBIS: 175; Edwards, Frank/Hulton Archive/Getty: 158; Eggers, Terry/CORBIS: Escott, Colin/Michael Ochs Archives/Getty: 26, epa/CORBIS: 75; Evans, Walker/CORBIS: 16; Evening Standard/Hulton Archive/Getty: 105; Fotos International/Hulton Archive/Getty: 107; Frank Driggs Collection/Hulton Archive/Getty: Back flap and 49; French, Gerald/CORBIS: 202; Galella, Ron/Wireimage/Getty: 186 and 191; Gehman, Raymond /CORBIS: Gould, Philip/CORBIS: 15; Hulton Archive/Getty: 8, 12, 42, 67 and 129; INTERFOTO Pressebildagentur/Alamy: 68; John Kobal Foundation/Hulton Archive/Getty: 50; John Springer Collection/CORBIS: Endpapers, 6, 48, 58, 60, 85r and 133; Kelley, Robert W./Time & Life Pictures/Getty: 25; Khan, Le Garsmeur, Alain/Alamy: 216t; Lockwood, Lee/Time & Life Pictures/Getty: 31; Magma Agency/Wireimage/Getty: 131; Mays, Buddy/CORBIS: 215; Memphis Brooks Museum/Michael Ochs Archives/Getty: 13 and 18; Michael Ochs Archives/CORBIS: 130; Michael Ochs Archives/Getty: Back cover, Front flap, 2, 5, 7, 9, 10, 17, 19t, 20, 22, 23, 28, 29, 35, 36r, 36, 37, 38, 40, 47, 57, 59, 61t, 62, 63, 65, 78, 99, 87, 88, 91, 95, 97, 121, 124, 139, 140, 141, 149, 150, 151, 157, 159, 162l, 162r, 163, 164, 167, 172, 173, 174, 178, 179, 185, 193, 195, 197, 199, 200, 208, 209, 214; Miller, Max B./Hulton Archive/Getty: 120; Moreland, Terrie/Michael Ochs Archives/Getty: 11; Paramount Pictures/Hulton Archive/Getty: 96 and 109; Photos 12/Alamy: 128; Photoshot/Hulton Archive/Getty: 108, 122; Pictorial Parade/Hulton Archive/Getty: 212; Pictorial Press Ltd/Alamy: 71, 127, 142, 144, 155, 177 and 205; Popperfoto/Getty: 100; Rastelli, Vittoriano/CORBIS: 74; Schulke, Flip/CORBIS: 145; Seattle Post-Intelligencer Collection/Museum of History and Industry/CORBIS: 104; Sunset Boulevard/CORBIS: 102, 111; The Print Collector/Alamy: 219; Underwood & Underwood/CORBIS: 19b and 184; Wargacki, Tom/Wireimage/Getty: 196, 198 and 201; Whitmore, James/Time & Life Pictures/Getty: 64, 77, and 106; Wright, Don/Time & Life Pictures/Getty: 45; Zlotnik, Charlyn / Michael Ochs Archives/Getty: 204t, and 204b.

Elvis Memorabillia

The Bridgewater Book Company would like to thank the King of Rock shop in the South Lanes, Brighton (UK) for the kind loan of record albums used in this book.

Every effort has been made to obtain permission to reproduce copyright material, but there may be cases where we have been unable to trace a copyright holder. The publisher will be happy to correct any omissions in the future printings.

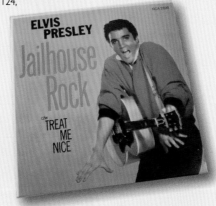